REPAIR & RENOVATE

windows&doors

REPAIR & RENOVATE

windows&doors

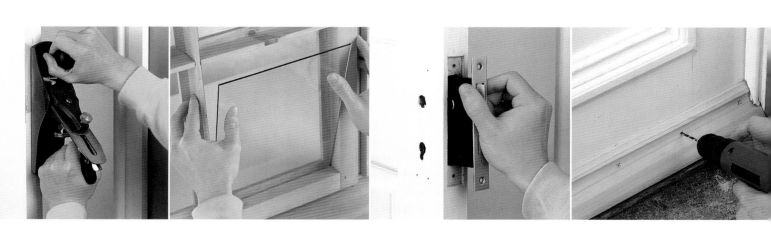

Julian Cassell & Peter Parham

MURDOCH BOOKS

20049763

windows & doors contents

*Locks and security fittings are vital components
on any exterior door, see page 68*

Painting a door requires some method in terms of order of work, see page 106 for practical advice

introduction

Home improvement is fast becoming a national pastime with more and more people tackling jobs that were previously left to the services of professional tradespeople. Taking on a job yourself can be more rewarding than hiring someone else and ensures that the finished effect is how you envisaged and falls within a budget that does not incur additional labour costs.

considering renovations

Windows and doors are an integral part of home make-up and design and because they are viewed on both the interior and exterior of the house, they play a key role in setting the style and finished look of your home. Deciding upon any sort of renovation related to these household features therefore requires lengthy consideration and a full evaluation of the effect any change will have.

Clearly, windows and doors are highly functional parts of a house but this must also be balanced with their design. To a certain degree, the emphasis on efficiency has been extended in modern times, as factors such as security and insulation have increased in importance. Manufacturers are always changing or making slight alterations to traditional styles in order to cater for these extra demands. Arguably, the most revolutionary of developments in the last couple of decades has been the introduction of double glazed units and pvc frames.

In the early years of their development, design or aesthetic properties were somewhat unimaginative with the emphasis firmly placed upon their functional capabilities. Now options are ever increasing and the market place is swamped with new ideas and designs, so you will almost certainly be able to find the most appropriate windows or doors tailored to your individual needs.

As always, personal choice and preference must be the most important considerations when choosing doors and windows. Of all the features in home layout, however, these are the items that tend to require some thought in terms of producing a well-balanced, rather than fragmented or random, look throughout the home.

With all renovation tasks, once decisions have been made concerning the projects to be undertaken, you will need to assess your capabilities and decide whether you are able to complete the entire job on your own or will need to seek professional advice.

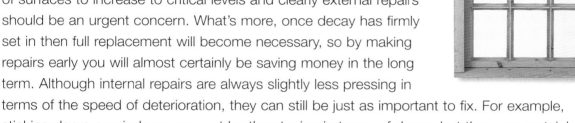

Total window replacement, replacing front doors or even changing internal doors can all be expensive projects, and even though you may carry out much of the work yourself, we all need to abide by certain budgetary constraints which should be set before any work begins. In many cases it may be more appropriate to turn attention to repairing windows and doors rather than full replacement, especially when you are happy with existing designs.

With external fixtures, weathering can cause deterioration of surfaces to increase to critical levels and clearly external repairs should be an urgent concern. What's more, once decay has firmly set in then full replacement will become necessary, so by making repairs early you will almost certainly be saving money in the long term. Although internal repairs are always slightly less pressing in terms of the speed of deterioration, they can still be just as important to fix. For example, sticking doors or windows may not be threatening in terms of decay, but they can certainly be considered high on the list of personal annoyances when going about day-to-day life!

In many cases, future repairs can be avoided by following the correct installation procedures. It may be that you have inherited problems caused by previous home-owners, but in those situations where you are installing new units, using the correct techniques will almost certainly reduce any future problems. Fitting hinges correctly, ensuring that new windows are weather proof, using the correct paints or natural wood finishes, are all examples of areas which if approached with a casual or even cavalier attitude at the outset will almost certainly cause problems further down the line. Following the right procedures for installing new materials detailed in this book will undoubtedly reduce repair needs in the long term.

Always remember that it is vital to follow the correct safety procedures

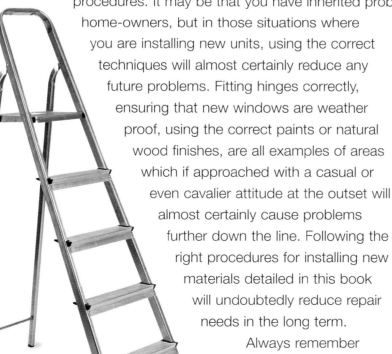

considering repairs & renovations

7

and use any necessary safety equipment for the particular task you are carrying out. All specific safety issues are dealt with in each chapter as the need arises, but it is always worth reinforcing the need for good working practices as far as safety is concerned, before you set out on any DIY task.

Windows and doors provide subjects of prime importance and concern when looking at issues of repair and renovation around your home. Whether you are working to improve their appearance, increase their efficiency, or a combination of both these factors, it is always worth remembering that such efforts are rarely ineffective. As well as increasing the value of your home, there can often be a far greater reward related to the overall look achieved and a quality of life for which you can take prime responsibility. In many ways home improvements are perceived as a chore, but there is always great benefit derived from seeing your own work admired.

The layout of this book has been designed to provide project instruction in as comprehensive yet straightforward a manner as possible. The illustration below provides a general guideline to the different elements incorporated into this design. Full colour photos and diagrams combined with explanatory text, laid out in a clear, step-by-step order, provide easy-to-follow instructions. Boxes of text aimed at drawing your attention to safety issues, general tips and alternative options accompany each project.

difficulty rating

The following symbols are designed to give an indication of difficulty level relating to particular tasks and projects in this book. Clearly what are simple jobs to one person may be difficult to another, and vice versa. These guidelines are primarily based on the ability of an individual in relation to the experience and degree of technical ability required.

Straightforward and requiring limited technical skills

Straightforward but requiring a reasonable skill level

Technically quite difficult, and could involve a number of skills

High skill level required and involves a number of techniques

safety boxes, coloured pink for emphasis, are designed to draw attention to the particular safety considerations for each project

tip boxes have been used to provide helpful hints, developed from professional experience, on how to achieve particular tasks

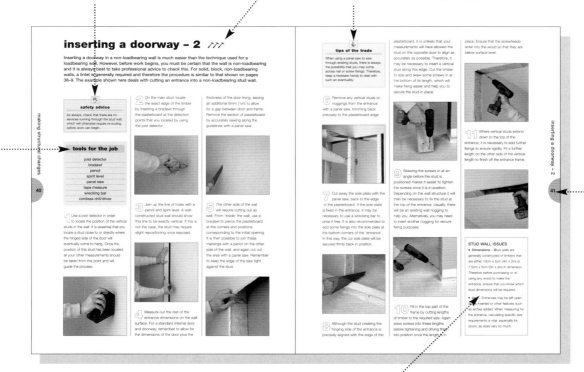

a list of tools has been provided at the beginning of each project

options boxes offer additonal instruction on techniques related to the project in hand

colour-coordinated tabs help you quickly find your place again when moving between chapters

anatomy of windows & doors

As with any structure in your home, the design and make-up of doors and windows will vary according to a number of factors. The age of your house, decisions taken by previous owners, your own particular preferences regarding appearance, and the specific function of the door or window will all affect the types of doors and windows you have in your home. Before making changes or restoring doors and windows, it is therefore necessary to have some understanding of the different structures which are available and how this relates to your own personal requirements. It is also important to determine how door and window structure relates to the walls they are fitted into, so that when change is implemented, you will have a good understanding of the work that is required to carry out particular tasks.

11

An arch window allows more light in and its curved outline will soften the overall look of any room.

door types & construction

There is a huge variation in door design, but they all have functions and features in common. Much of the structural variation derives from the materials used. This in turn is related to cost and so, to a certain degree, structure and quality are common denominators in the design of doors. The examples given here provide a cross section of door types and help towards understanding the differences in door design.

solid panel doors

Wooden panel doors are very common and manufactured in a wide range of qualities. Softwood varieties are much less expensive than hardwood doors, the latter commonly being used for front doors.

top panels may be glazed rather than solid wood – a common option in hardwood front doors

mortice and tenon joint

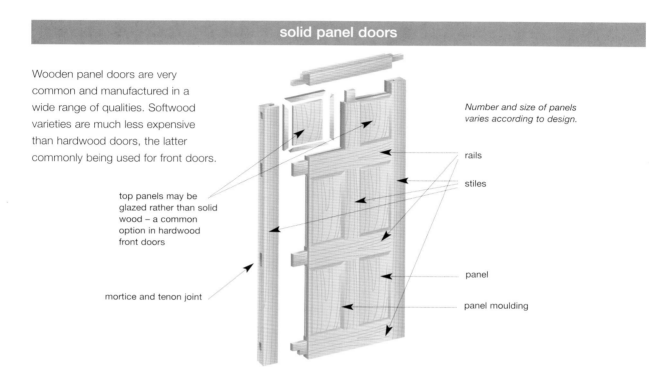

Number and size of panels varies according to design.

rails

stiles

panel

panel moulding

ledge & brace doors

This more traditional and 'rustic' door design offers a completely different look. The construction is based on a number of different timber sections attached vertically and braced by horizontal and diagonal rails.

Sometimes ledged and braced doors are framed with rails and stiles to make a more substantial structure.

Hinges will be surface mounted on ledges. Those used are not butt hinges but T-hinges (for example, see antique iron hinge page 54).

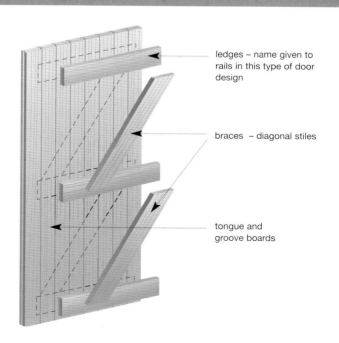

ledges – name given to rails in this type of door design

braces – diagonal stiles

tongue and groove boards

flush door (solid)

Solid flush doors have plain flat surfaces without any sort of panel features. The materials used in their construction do vary, but the framework of the door is usually made from softwood timbers and the actual door surface from ply.

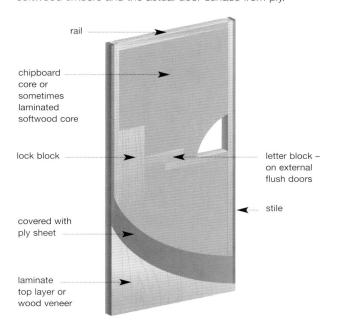

rail

chipboard core or sometimes laminated softwood core

lock block

letter block – on external flush doors

covered with ply sheet

stile

laminate top layer or wood veneer

flush door (hollow)

These cheaper versions of solid flush doors tend only to be used internally and offer an economical option for fitting new doors throughout your home. Though less substantial, they can still be used very effectively.

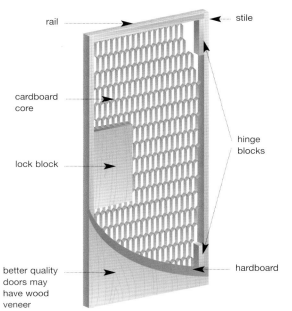

rail

stile

cardboard core

hinge blocks

lock block

better quality doors may have wood veneer

hardboard

pvc doors

These doors tend to be used in homes where double glazing and good insulation are a priority. They are moulded and supplied with a fitted frame, ready for installation into a wall aperture. Generally used only as external doors.

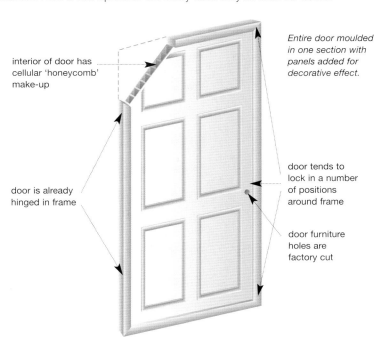

interior of door has cellular 'honeycomb' make-up

Entire door moulded in one section with panels added for decorative effect.

door is already hinged in frame

door tends to lock in a number of positions around frame

door furniture holes are factory cut

tips of the trade

Softwood – Most warping problems occur with softwood doors. Therefore, there is a tendency for most exterior wooden doors to be hardwood. Although softwood doors can be used for external use, be sure to buy good quality decorating materials in these cases which will then ensure that the wood is treated with the best possible exterior decorating system.

safety advice

Fire considerations – Before purchasing a new door it is worth considering what regulations the door conforms to. This is especially important when turning attention to its performance in the event of a fire. Some doors are specifically supplied as 'fire doors' because retardant materials are built into their design. It is therefore important to check these issues and consider their relevance to your needs before making a final choice.

how doors are fitted

All doors are fitted into some form of frame or lining, and differences tend to lie in the hinging mechanism and how it works in relation to the frame. Fitting mechanisms also tend to be slightly different for internal doors compared to external doors. This factor also relates to the differing door structures in each case. The illustrations provided identify many of the themes which differ between internal doors and how this affects their relationship to the frame or lining.

internal doors

In this example, a solid wood panel door has been used for illustrative purposes. However, most of the features and mechanisms referred to can be related to other kinds of internal doors. For example, although many flush doors have hollow areas in their structure, the actual door perimeter is solid so that hinges and opening mechanisms may be fitted.

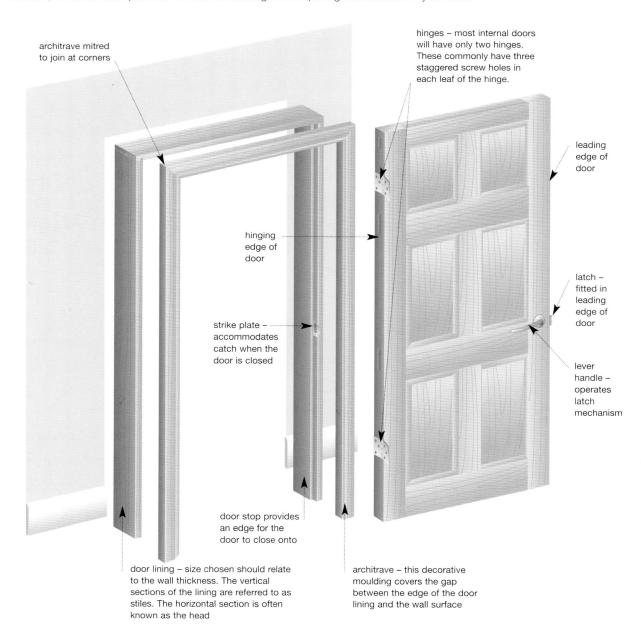

architrave mitred to join at corners

hinges – most internal doors will have only two hinges. These commonly have three staggered screw holes in each leaf of the hinge.

leading edge of door

hinging edge of door

latch – fitted in leading edge of door

strike plate – accommodates catch when the door is closed

lever handle – operates latch mechanism

door stop provides an edge for the door to close onto

door lining – size chosen should relate to the wall thickness. The vertical sections of the lining are referred to as stiles. The horizontal section is often known as the head

architrave – this decorative moulding covers the gap between the edge of the door lining and the wall surface

External doors tend to have slightly more features than internal doors, as security becomes more of an issue and the door incorporates structures aimed at counteracting the weathering process.

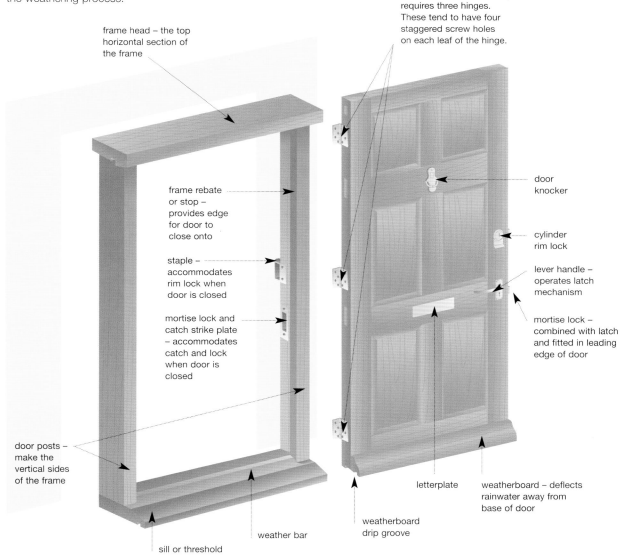

hinges – the extra weight of an external door usually requires three hinges. These tend to have four staggered screw holes on each leaf of the hinge.

frame head – the top horizontal section of the frame

frame rebate or stop – provides edge for door to close onto

staple – accommodates rim lock when door is closed

mortise lock and catch strike plate – accommodates catch and lock when door is closed

door posts – make the vertical sides of the frame

sill or threshold

weather bar

door knocker

cylinder rim lock

lever handle – operates latch mechanism

mortise lock – combined with latch and fitted in leading edge of door

letterplate

weatherboard drip groove

weatherboard – deflects rainwater away from base of door

patio doors

Other common varieties of external door include patio doors. These are sometimes hinged or in many cases are positioned in runners and are therefore opened and closed by a sliding mechanism. In both cases the frame of the door itself is fitted into the wall in a similar manner to any exterior door. In other words, the frame is fixed in the wall aperture and then the doors added. Before purchasing, check that any patio doors you choose have good security features.

garage doors

Garage doors, although completely different in terms of size and style to other forms of external door, do still follow similar fitting principles, with the frame still being fitted before the door is hung. It is at the later stages where variations can occur, because although many garage doors are hinged in a similar position to normal exterior doors, others have automatic opening mechanisms which require completely different fitting techniques.

window types & construction

Much of the variation between window types relates to style and period. There is also a need to consider window function in terms of insulatory properties, and to what extent opening lights and casements are required in the window structure. The examples provided here help to demonstrate many of the variations available and to show the major differences in the construction of each type of window.

casements

The term 'casements' generally refers to windows with hinged opening sections combined with fixed sections. The design within this category can therefore vary considerably (see choosing options pp.80–81).

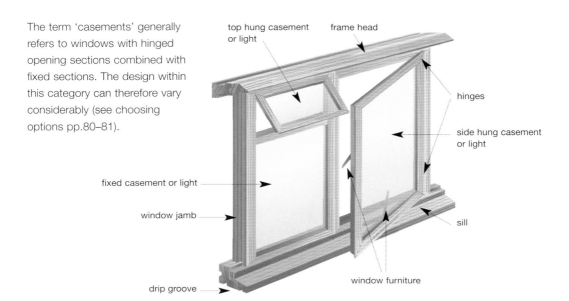

top hung casement or light

frame head

hinges

side hung casement or light

fixed casement or light

window jamb

sill

drip groove

window furniture

sashes

These are traditional-looking windows, which involve the movement of casements or lights in the window frame by means of a cord and pulley mechanism. Modern variations may use chains or have spiral balances.

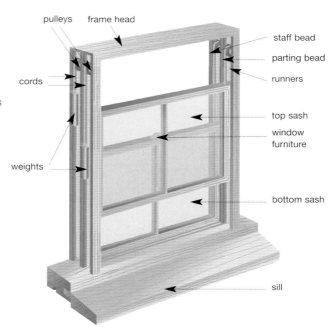

pulleys

frame head

staff bead

parting bead

runners

cords

top sash

window furniture

weights

bottom sash

sill

roof windows

These vary considerably in design from normal windows and are based on the principle that they fit into a pitched roof situation. Tiles are removed and the window is positioned or cut into the roof timbers, with the addition of some extra support.

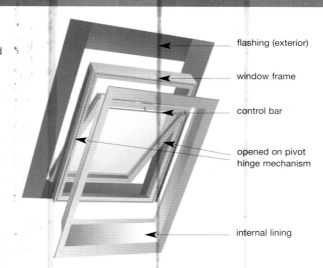

flashing (exterior)

window frame

control bar

opened on pivot hinge mechanism

internal lining

bay windows

Bay windows are large windows which extend out from the front of a house, often positioned on either side of the front door or entrance. Structure tends to take the form of a casement window which has been stuck together in a number of sections.

separate components fixed together to complete shape of window

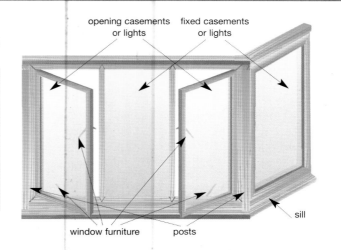

opening casements or lights

fixed casements or lights

window furniture

posts

sill

pvc windows

These windows provide by far the best insulation and can take the form of either casement or sash, depending on the manufacturer's design. As a result of its thermal efficiency and low maintenance requirement, this structure has become increasingly popular for homeowners.

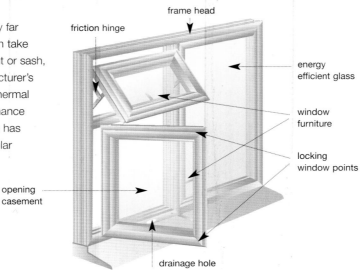

frame head

friction hinge

energy efficient glass

window furniture

locking window points

opening casement

drainage hole

how windows are fitted

Broadly speaking, the main determining factor in the positioning of windows is whether the wall in which they are to be fitted is of a solid or cavity structure. The former situation tends to apply to older houses where solid walls are more prevalent, whereas a cavity wall situation is more likely to be found in modern houses. The general issues for both are outlined here, showing the most important features relevant to the fitting of windows in these two common wall structures.

solid walls

Most new houses are built with a cavity wall structure, but if you need to replace windows in older properties it is necessary to understand how they are fitted so that replacement may be carried out using the correct technique. The main difference here relates to the fact that in older properties, where there is no cavity, it is unlikely that a DPC ('damp proof course') was used around the window. Therefore replacement merely requires positioning the window in the same place as the previous one was situated. Once the window is in place, the junction between frame and masonry is sealed with mortar and sealant.

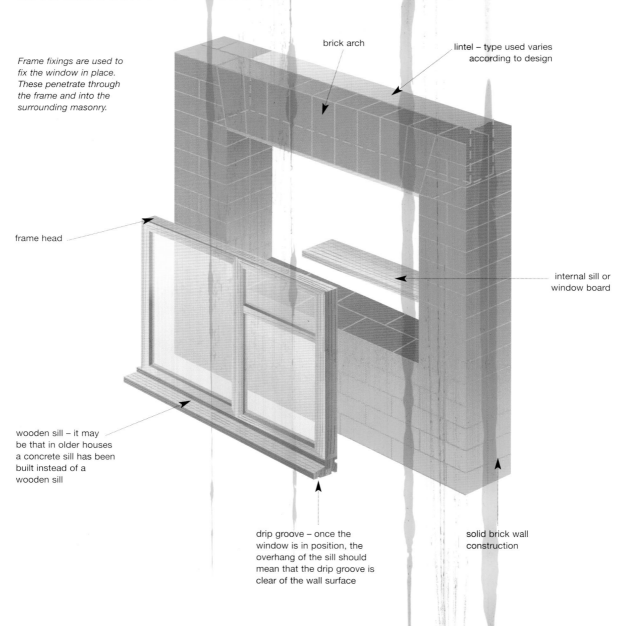

Frame fixings are used to fix the window in place. These penetrate through the frame and into the surrounding masonry.

brick arch

lintel – type used varies according to design

frame head

internal sill or window board

wooden sill – it may be that in older houses a concrete sill has been built instead of a wooden sill

drip groove – once the window is in position, the overhang of the sill should mean that the drip groove is clear of the wall surface

solid brick wall construction

With cavity walls, positioning is slightly different and different factors need taking into account when looking at how the window is fixed in position. There will inevitably be slight variations depending on window type but this illustration helps demonstrate the main principles involved. Whether the window is wooden, pvc or metal, similar principles of fixing are used.

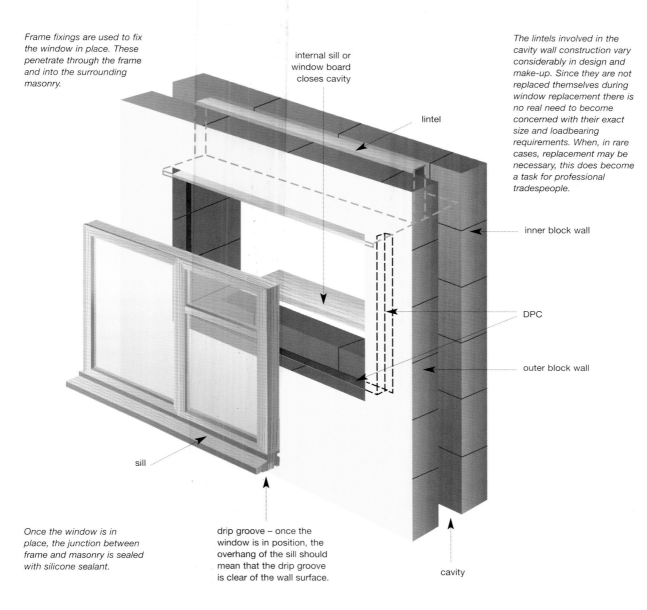

Frame fixings are used to fix the window in place. These penetrate through the frame and into the surrounding masonry.

internal sill or window board closes cavity

lintel

The lintels involved in the cavity wall construction vary considerably in design and make-up. Since they are not replaced themselves during window replacement there is no real need to become concerned with their exact size and loadbearing requirements. When, in rare cases, replacement may be necessary, this does become a task for professional tradespeople.

inner block wall

DPC

outer block wall

sill

Once the window is in place, the junction between frame and masonry is sealed with silicone sealant.

drip groove – once the window is in position, the overhang of the sill should mean that the drip groove is clear of the wall surface.

cavity

bay windows

Although bay windows display many similar characteristics in the way they are fitted, it is important to realise that in some situations the bay window itself does have a weight-supporting and therefore loadbearing part to play in house structure. Simply taking out an old bay window and replacing it with a new one should only be undertaken once the relevant checks have been made. Therefore if you are thinking of replacing a bay window, it is always best to seek some professional advice, thus making sure that you take any measures needed to support the wall structure.

formers

In modern houses it is not uncommon to find an extra part to the framing structure of a window. This extra piece is called a former and is inserted, or more accurately, built into the wall structure to create the correct size of opening for the window to be fitted into.

glass & glazing options

Glass options need a certain amount of consideration as clearly all windows contain some sort of glass, along with many part glazed or totally glazed doors. Modern invention and innovation has allowed for a range of different types of glass to become available, with differing properties of both their finish and function. Decisions therefore need to be made on what type of glass is suitable for your needs in relation to the door or window in question.

clear glass

By far the most common type of glass used in houses is clear, to allow the maximum amount of light into the house and to ensure the view outside is made as clear and open as possible. However, clear glass can in itself be divided into a number of categories which are difficult to pick up instantly with the naked eye.

thickness

Glass thickness is often difficult to spot when it is in position and only when you see the edges of glass panes does it become apparent that there can be considerable variation. In general, thinner clear glass is used for windows and thicker versions are used in doors. This tends to relate to safety considerations, as thinner glass is naturally easier to break and therefore a child mistakenly running into a glass door is less likely to break the glass and cause injury. As well as being thicker, glass used in doors and low-level areas in the home should also be safety glass or toughened, so that if it is broken it shatters into relatively small granular sections which tend not to cause injury compared to the sharper shards common in normal glass breakages.

laminated glass

Laminated glass is in fact two or more panes of glass which have a clear plastic layer fused in between them. This plastic layer binds the panes together as one solid structure. It is available in many different thicknesses and varieties such as clear, patterned and tinted. Laminated glass is difficult to cut and it is therefore advisable to get glass cut to size by your supplier. Although laminated glass is an expensive option, it is an excellent choice in security terms as well as for safety purposes – in glazed doors, for example. It can absorb greater impact than most alternatives and is therefore relatively strong. If it does break under severe impact, the plastic layer holds the glass pieces in position so that it remains in one piece and splinters of glass are not spread all around.

double glazed units

Double glazed units are two panes of glass separated by a void filled with inert gas and then totally sealed off from the surrounding atmosphere. Glass thickness tends to increase according to pane size and so the larger the panes, the thicker the glass. Double glazed units may be fitted into pvc and aluminium framed windows as well as new wooden ones. However, if you wish to change single panes for double glazed units in an existing window, you will need to check that the rebates in the frame are wide enough to accommodate the new unit. If they are too narrow, it will be necessary to fit units with a stepped edge to allow for the difference. Double glazed units significantly improve insulation and can reduce condensation as well as noise pollution.

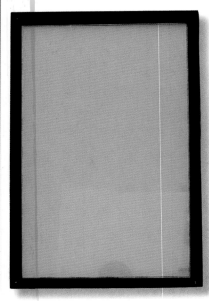

patterned clear glass

Patterned clear glass is often used in a modesty or privacy function. For example, bathroom windows or doors may contain such glass to provide the required privacy whilst still allowing maximum light into the room. With a wide range of designs available, there is considerable room for choice and thus for finding a suitable option for your own personal requirements.

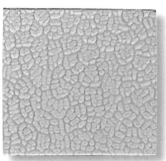 

patterned coloured glass

Coloured patterned glass offers a further design option and is often used in conjunction with clear patterned glass when maximum light requirement is not a priority.

lead lights

Lead lights provide a traditional looking window and are often supplied using different coloured glass in varying designs. They can be fitted into appropriately designed casements or are common features in part-glazed front doors. Many companies will provide a 'self design' service allowing you to decide which you require.

etched glass

Etched glass can be considered a more exclusive version of patterned glass and is more commonly used in part-glazed front doors. As well as adding privacy, light is still let in and the availability and attractiveness of designs makes this option a real addition to the overall look of windows or doors.

wired glass

Wired glass has a mesh inside the glass pane to increase its strength, even though the glass itself may still shatter when broken. It is not particularly attractive and tends only to be used in fire doors because of its retardant properties. The wire binds the glass together during a fire and therefore maintains a retardant barrier.

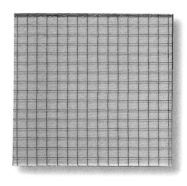

planning

When considering repair or renovation tasks, planning is an essential part of any project and relates to more than just the practical side of carrying out the proposed work. Firstly, decisions concerning the exact changes you wish to implement need careful consideration before any projects may commence. Other areas for concern include having the correct tools and materials for the job, working out the best strategy for the particular project and taking into account issues such as planning permission and building regulations. An awareness and understanding of these other factors are a necessary requirement for any building project, and this chapter takes these factors into account and explains how they relate to different tasks around the home. Attention to detail at this crucial stage will inevitably result in the smooth running of any repair or renovation.

Glass panels on connecting doors help link two different living spaces and encourage the free flow of light.

options for change

Work on windows and doors may have aesthetic consequences for both the interior and exterior of your home. Therefore, when looking at options for change or different styles in general, it is important to bear this point in mind so that your final selection fulfils both criteria. Similarly, doors and windows must also be chosen to complement other design factors in a room and, in the case of window replacement, external architecture and design clearly need to be taken into account.

traditional exteriors

In older properties, being sympathetic to historical features and design is clearly important, and, if the building is listed, it may be subject to planning controls. However, in most cases of this nature, trying to keep style authentic is the aim of renovation and therefore replacing doors or windows to match the existing style is normally the adopted approach. So whether completely replacing a door or window, carrying out repairs, or merely re-decorating, issues of authenticity should always be addressed.

RIGHT *Front doors are a focal point for most homes and should therefore be in good decorative order. Ensuring that they function efficiently is vital when they are in daily use.*

double glazing

Double glazing is fast becoming the norm, especially in modern buildings. The practical advantages make this option extremely popular and have given rise to a huge industry, which tackles both installation in new properties and replacement in older ones. There are strong personal opinions and preferences when it comes to choosing this option, but it must be understood that up-to-date designs of double glazing are far superior to earlier styles, which often lacked imagination or any concern for taste and architecture. Therefore, if you find the correct manufacturer, today's double glazed units can be far more sympathetic to personal and design requirements.

LEFT *Modern double glazing designs can be tailored to individual needs, providing all the benefits of low maintenance and insulation without changing the basic character of older properties.*

modern interiors

In many modern homes, window or door design is kept to minimalist levels in that they are treated as purely practical features. Large panes of glass maximize the amount of light that is available and modern door designs place an emphasis on simplicity and plainness. However, this purely practical look does in itself evoke a style that focuses on other room details and allows practical items, such as doors and windows, to act as backdrops rather than highlighted or over-emphasized features.

traditional interiors

Traditional or highly styled interiors require a great deal of attention when it comes to planning renovation work. The design of the doors and windows tends to be more interesting and intricate than modern equivalents, often making them strong features in their own right. They can either be highlighted with bold colours or the actual design itself can often add a decorative aspect.

ABOVE RIGHT *In a modern, uncluttered interior, simple window design often provides the most practical and attractive option.*

MIDDLE RIGHT *A pair of heavy and ornate doors evokes both a welcoming and grand atmosphere in a traditional hallway.*

BELOW *A curving 'wall' of windows provides an unusual design element as well as an excellent option for letting in light.*

unusual interiors

There is clearly a large area or category somewhere between traditional and modern designs of doors and windows that allows for greater expression of personal taste. In fact, highly individual approaches to choosing door and window design are often the preferred option, and the method of decoration can add a particular accent to more unusual door and window choices.

tools & equipment

The range of tools and equipment necessary for completing DIY tasks can be vast and expensive. Yet many of the basic tools are in fact multi-purpose, and make up what might be called a 'household tool kit'. Once this strong base of essential tools has been established, you can go on to purchase more specialized tools as and when they are required. Although it is not necessary to spend a fortune, it is generally a good rule to buy the best tools that you can afford.

household tools

This general household tool kit contains the essential tools for carrying out small jobs and tasks around the home. Although the kit will not cope with every situation you encounter, it provides a good starting point to which you can add more specific tool requirements.

claw hammer

sanding block

wire brush

slot-head screwdrivers

cross-head screwdrivers

insulated sleeves

nail punch

pipe, joist and cable detector

craft knife

combination pliers

bradawl

carpenter's pencil

side cutters

long-nose pliers

half-round rasp

general purpose chisels

cordless drill/driver

oil stone

plier wrench

sealant dispenser

stepladder

clamp

wooden mallet

tape measure

mini hacksaw

mini level

scraper

mitre block

panel saw

power tools

Power tools are designed to make jobs easier and less time consuming. For most enthusiasts, mid-range tools are ideal, as the very expensive equipment is designed for everyday work, and the very cheap equipment for the occasional DIY person. Even so, the cost of power tools has dropped considerably, and it is possible to buy quality products relatively cheaply. For some tasks, it can even be worth buying very cheap tools for limited use before discarding.

power drill

router

jigsaw

electric sander

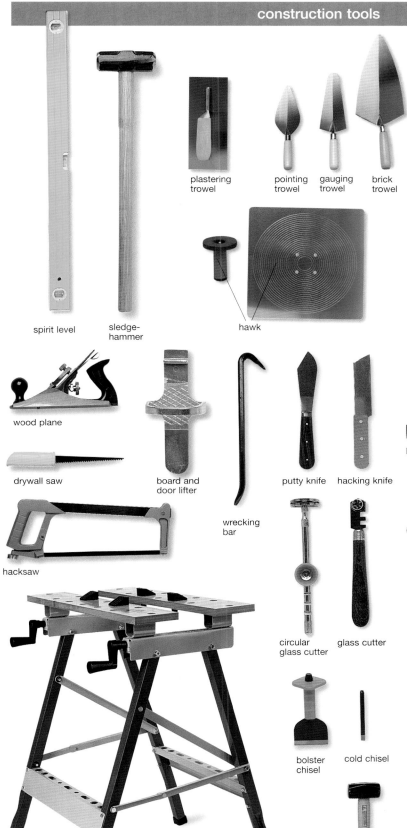

spirit level

sledge-hammer

plastering trowel

pointing trowel

gauging trowel

brick trowel

hawk

In order to carry out alterations to windows and doors, the household tool kit needs to be supplemented with construction tools for heavy duty tasks, and other tools designed specifically with the renovation or installation of doors and windows in mind. Try to concentrate on specific needs when purchasing such tools, as it can be tempting to fall for gimmicky options or cheap alternatives that will be of minimal use in the long term. Instead, stick to good quality, tried and tested tools which should last for several years of DIY projects. If you are unsure of the best product, consult your retailer.

plastic bucket

wood plane

drywall saw

board and door lifter

wrecking bar

putty knife

hacking knife

butt marker

circular glass cutter

glass cutter

hacksaw

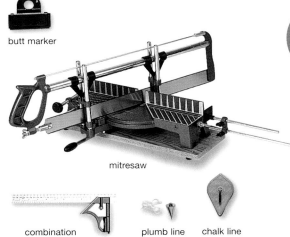

mitresaw

combination square

plumb line

chalk line

bolster chisel

cold chisel

workbench

club hammer

HIRING TOOLS

For isolated tasks that require particularly heavy duty equipment, or tools that are very expensive to buy, hiring is often the best option. This area has become a growing sector of the DIY market, and hire shops are increasingly catering for home repair enthusiasts, as well as traditional trade customers.

fixings & materials

In order to renovate windows and doors, it is necessary to use a selection of materials for general fixing and fitting purposes. Actual requirements will clearly depend on the type of repair you are effecting or whether you are actually fitting new units as a whole. Therefore, it is important to have some awareness of material requirements so that they can be purchased as needed directly for the job at hand. Remember that suppliers will generally give good advice on particular materials needed.

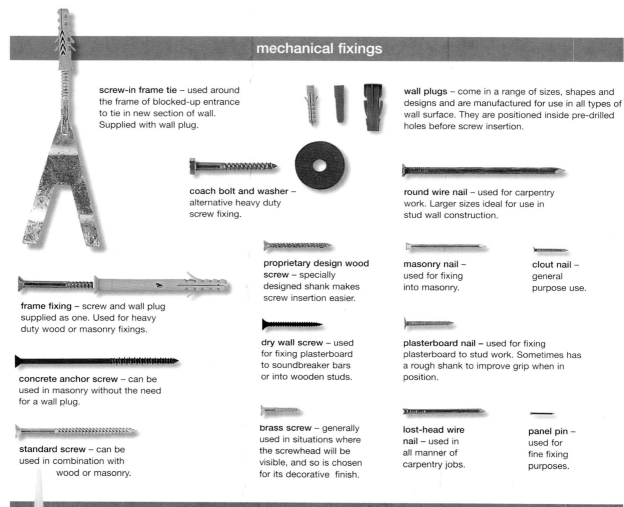

mechanical fixings

screw-in frame tie – used around the frame of blocked-up entrance to tie in new section of wall. Supplied with wall plug.

wall plugs – come in a range of sizes, shapes and designs and are manufactured for use in all types of wall surface. They are positioned inside pre-drilled holes before screw insertion.

coach bolt and washer – alternative heavy duty screw fixing.

round wire nail – used for carpentry work. Larger sizes ideal for use in stud wall construction.

frame fixing – screw and wall plug supplied as one. Used for heavy duty wood or masonry fixings.

proprietary design wood screw – specially designed shank makes screw insertion easier.

masonry nail – used for fixing into masonry.

clout nail – general purpose use.

concrete anchor screw – can be used in masonry without the need for a wall plug.

dry wall screw – used for fixing plasterboard to soundbreaker bars or into wooden studs.

plasterboard nail – used for fixing plasterboard to stud work. Sometimes has a rough shank to improve grip when in position.

standard screw – can be used in combination with wood or masonry.

brass screw – generally used in situations where the screwhead will be visible, and so is chosen for its decorative finish.

lost-head wire nail – used in all manner of carpentry jobs.

panel pin – used for fine fixing purposes.

fillers, sealants & tapes

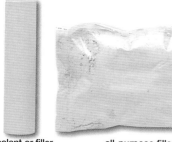

sealant or filler tubes – many sealants or flexible fillers are supplied in a tubed form. Sealant gun required to expel material from tube.

all-purpose filler – multi-purpose filler, mixed with water to create 'paste' for filling holes in most surfaces.

jointing compound – supplied ready mixed. Used for filling over taped joints and nail heads when dry lining.

self-adhesive jointing tape – used to cover joins between plasterboard sheets. Easy to apply.

masking tape – used to mask surfaces before decoration or to temporarily hold lightweight objects in position.

insulating tape – multi-purpose pvc tape.

adhesives

plasticizer – additive to mortar to improve mortar mixture ease of use.

wood glue – for sticking together wooden surfaces.

pva – multi-purpose adhesive used in concentrated or dilute forms.

bonding & finishing materials

bonding coat – water added, and used as heavy duty filler prior to plastering.

undercoat plaster – water added and used as undercoat to multi-finish plaster.

cement – added to water with sand to create mortar for building purposes. Other general uses.

one-coat plaster – water added and used as general purpose plaster.

multi-finish plaster – water added and used as top coat finishing plaster.

building sand – added to cement and water to create mortar for building purposes.

construction materials

sawn softwood 10cm x 5cm (4in x 2in) – multi-purpose building material.

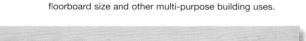

prepared softwood 12.5cm x 2.5cm (5in x 1in) – common floorboard size and other multi-purpose building uses.

prepared softwood 5cm x 2.5cm (2in x 1in) – used for frameworks for cladding or plasterboarding.

panel moulding – decorative feature added to flush doors to create a panelled effect.

architrave – decorative trim around doorways. Available in all sizes and many designs.

skirting board – decorative and protective trim at floor/wall junction. Available in all sizes and many designs.

pre-formed plaster arch – used as fixed template for forming arched entrances or openings.

angle bead – metal former used to create precise external corners when plastering.

medium density fibreboard – better known as mdf, used as a general purpose building board. Manufactured in various thicknesses and varieties.

plasterboard – manufactured in various thicknesses and varieties. Used as a base for plaster or dry lined finishes.

how to start

The order of work for starting renovation on doors and windows is highly dependent on whether you are carrying out repairs, considering total replacement or whether the work is part of a larger renovation project, which opens up further avenues for consideration. It is, therefore, necessary to look at all of these options within a framework that can account for the majority of potential repair or renovation possibilities and scenarios. Careful planning at this stage will save time later on.

planning permission

Before any construction project can begin, some consideration must be given to whether the particular work will need planning permission. The majority of projects inside the home do not need planning approval, and so this is not an issue for most works that you are likely to carry out. However, there are some circumstances which you should be aware of before beginning renovations.

restrictions

Most restrictions are applied to houses that are listed buildings and/or are in conservation areas, national parks, or areas of outstanding natural beauty. If your property fits into any of these categories, always call the local authority planning department before commencing any plans.

However, even in these cases, formal permission is rarely required for internal alterations, minor improvements, and general repairs and maintenance. Projects that definitely require planning permission are generally those in which an area of the house has a 'change of use', normally when business purposes are proposed. For example, if you wish to divide off a section of your home for business use, or you want to create a separate bedsit or flat. So generally speaking, in addition to the restrictions mentioned here, as long as the external appearance of the building is not changed, internal work may be carried out relatively free from too many planning obstacles. However, if you are in any doubt about what is permissible, it is best to contact your local authority.

External work can sometimes be subject to strict building restrictions. Always check with an appropriate body before embarking on work that may require authorization.

building regulations

While most internal renovation is unlikely to require actual planning permission, all construction work should adhere to building regulations. So whenever you plan to carry out any construction work, contact the Building Control Officer at your local council, who can provide any necessary guidelines for potential work.

making a scale drawing

It is always sensible to make a scale drawing of a proposed construction job, in order to get a firm idea of material quantities. This does not have to be up to architectural standards, but it should provide enough detail to give you a good idea of the effect a project will have, and how it will change the existing look of your home. Graph paper always makes any technical drawing easier, and allows for more accurate measurement. It can often be helpful to add furniture to the diagram, so that you can gauge the effect of the alteration on the overall layout of the room – this can be especially important when dividing an existing room into two separate areas, as the amount of space is obviously reduced.

timescales

Always consider the timescale required to complete a project, as this can influence the most convenient time to commence the job. For example, while some projects can be completed in a weekend, other jobs will take longer, causing disruption to the household for several days. Most projects in this book are designed to be completed within a weekend, although you will need to return to the job for final

Many DIY tasks will cause some inevitable disruption to the household. Bear this in mind when planning a job, and aim to commence work at a time convenient to all of those involved.

Making a scale drawing can help you to visualize the effect of any work on the surrounding environment. Adding furniture to the diagram will also help.

finishing and decorating, which may mean it takes a little longer. As soon as you begin to combine a number of projects, or work on large areas, completing jobs can become more difficult. This is especially true of projects that run between weekends or evenings, so it is advisable either to break them down into smaller sections which can be completed as part of an overall larger renovation, or take time away from day-to-day work in order to make headway into the particular task and minimize disruption. Otherwise, pressure to finish the job can lead to inadequate work with poor finishing. Never underestimate the time involved in a project, and consider it an important part of the planning procedure to decide on dates and times when the work can be done, and within what timescale it can be finished.

budgeting

The greatest expense in a construction project is usually the price of the labour itself, and therefore by reducing this input, costs are reduced. If professional trades are required, this should be given priority in terms of your overall budgeting strategy. Aside from this, material costs can be calculated relatively easily so long as accurate measurements are taken. Remember that bulk buying of particular materials should mean financial discounts, and it is always worth shopping around for the best deals. This is especially the case with common items such as general timber and plasterboard because the market is so competitive, and suppliers can vary their prices from week to week. If your planning is comprehensive, you have a better chance of remaining within your budget. However, it is always worth building in a slight surplus requirement to your figures so that if work does take longer – or require more materials – you are able to complete the project without delay.

dealing with professionals

Prior to any construction work, you need to establish what work you are personally capable of and to what extent you will require professional help. Small renovations or repairs are unlikely to need much assistance, but in tackling major renovation you will almost certainly need to call upon the services of plumbers, electricians or general builders. In which case, you should try to identify the kinds of assistance required and understand how to get the best service out of tradespeople.

architects & surveyors

In some circumstances it may be necessary to draw on the services of architects and surveyors. Although not considered 'tradespeople', they supply services that enable the practical side of major renovations to be planned and carried out in the correct manner. Architects only really need employing on ambitious projects where major design features have to be considered and plans drawn up. Or you might like to employ an architect or surveyor on large projects in more of a project management role, in order to oversee general work. Bear in mind that these services cost money and fees for monitoring work can add a further 10% to the original cost of drawing up plans. So only go down the architect or surveyor route if you feel it is absolutely necessary and you have available funds.

Professional advice for major projects is always a good idea, particularly for projects that may require planning permission. Bear these costs in mind when planning the work.

finding good tradespeople

The first major hurdle when using tradespeople in your home is to find those who are both capable and reliable. If you are choosing through advertisements, selecting from three or four quotations rather than one at random will only increase the probability of finding a good tradesperson by a very small amount. Nor are trade association badges a sure guarantee of worthiness in many cases. If you are influenced by such signs then check out their credentials, both with the association itself and with an independent body. By far the best method is to guarantee the quality of a tradesperson's work before employing them by seeing or hearing about it first hand. This can be done through personal recommendation by a friend or neighbour, or simply by asking to look at any building work going on in your local area, contacting the property owner or builder direct.

estimates, quotations & prices

Before allowing any tradesperson to begin work in your home, it is essential to know how much the job is going to cost. Here you encounter the potential minefield of estimates, quotations and prices. The main factor to bear in mind at this stage is that if you receive an estimate or a quotation, then this is exactly what it is, an estimate or quotation – the price that you actually end up paying could inflate considerably. If possible, it is therefore best to pin a tradesperson down to a price, for unless you change specifications for the work this should be the figure you pay at the end of the job. In some circumstances, an estimate may be necessary, as you yourself may not have made final decisions on specifications and need to see how the project develops. However, the closer you can get to deciding on a price before the work begins, the better position you will find yourself in when budgeting for the job and keeping track of payments. On the issue of payment, never make the mistake of paying any money up front unless there are exceptional circumstances. For example, if the tradesperson is supplying expensive materials, it is only fair that you should make an initial down payment towards the cost of those materials. Otherwise there is no reason to pay until the

Keep the lines of communication open. Although the cost of work may rise slightly as the job progresses, this can be negotiated at each stage, helping you monitor the cost overall.

job is complete and you are happy with the finished product. For long projects, it is fair to stage payments throughout its course, but always leave the largest payment until completion. Finally, treat builders or tradespeople who insist on cash only payments with some suspicion. Although there are potential savings to be made in this line, it means you have no comeback in terms of defective work or problems at a later date. Not to mention the potential illegality of such action in the eyes of the tax authorities.

extras

On making any final payment, seeing the word 'extras' or 'extra work carried out' can add a surprising shock, and indeed figure, to the amount you were expecting to pay. In many cases, these may be items that you authorized during the overall works, but in this situation it is always best to get a price for extra work before it is done, so that shocks do not occur at the final stage of payment. Alternatively, build a clause into the initial estimate that covers extra work, which is only to be carried out on your authority and which is charged at a specific hourly rate. Therefore, it is much easier to keep track of expenses, and the money does not simply add up without you being aware of it.

avoiding disputes

Disputes can be avoided quite simply as long as you follow the recognized 'rules of engagement'. Over half the battle is won if you have chosen the right tradesperson. Further gains can be made by ensuring that the price you receive is written and detailed in terms of the work to be carried out. This therefore acts as an accurate referral document for all parties. Aside from this, the only problems that really arise are if the work hasn't been carried out to a satisfactory standard or is actually different to what was initially agreed. Most of these problems can be sorted out through discussion and compromise, and it is best to avoid going down legal channels unless absolutely necessary. If you are very unhappy with the work carried out, then your only option may be to withhold payment and hand the matter over to solicitors.

If you follow these guidelines, you should be well equipped to consider the use of different tradespeople in your home. Simply remember that in all occupations there are both good and bad operators, and the building business gets more than its fair share of criticism. However, if you do have a reliable tradesperson at your disposable, pay them on time, recommend them to friends, and in looking after their interests, you will certainly be looking after your own.

Professional tradespeople will do a good job for a fair price. However, before agreeing on the terms and conditions of the contract, establish the length of time and expense of the project.

making structural changes

When carrying out work that requires structural change in your home, you will always need to give careful consideration to ensure that building regulations are being adhered to, and that proper attention is given to whether the changes you are making are concerned with loadbearing or non-loadbearing walls. This chapter explains these areas of concern and looks at the best ways of tackling such structural changes. Most of the examples provided here refer to work on internal walls and are therefore more relevant to the renovation of doors than windows. Although inserting a new window into a wall is sometimes a renovation that non-professionals carry out, it is best to draw a line here in terms of the capability of home improvement enthusiasts. It is advisable to leave this sort of work to the professionals – the more straightforward replacement of an existing window fixture is tackled in chapter 5.

Arch profiles provide a more relaxed type of division between rooms than traditional door fixtures.

safety at work

Any repair or renovation work must always be conducted employing the necessary safety procedures. This involves purchasing a certain amount of safety equipment, and an understanding of the best techniques for gaining access to high areas and the correct ways of using such access equipment. Remember when choosing safety equipment that it is important to purchase only those items that display the relevant safety standard markings.

first aid kit

By far the greatest number of injuries resulting from home improvement are very minor grazes and abrasions, and therefore it is essential to have a well stocked first aid kit in your home.

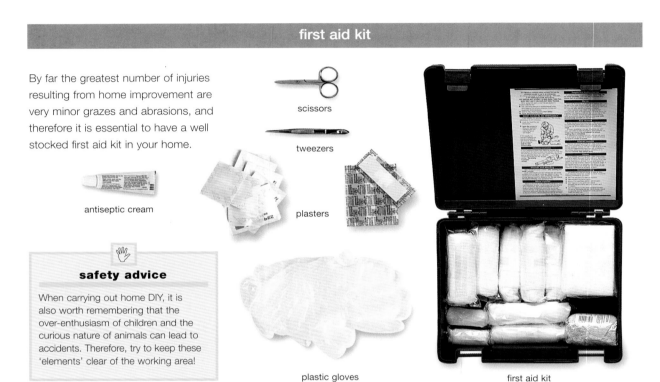

scissors

tweezers

antiseptic cream

plasters

safety advice

When carrying out home DIY, it is also worth remembering that the over-enthusiasm of children and the curious nature of animals can lead to accidents. Therefore, try to keep these 'elements' clear of the working area!

plastic gloves

first aid kit

safety equipment

A range of safety equipment is available for various DIY tasks. Some items are intended for particular jobs, but many pieces, such as work boots, goggles and protective gloves, should be worn in most situations.

dust mask

protective gloves

knee pads

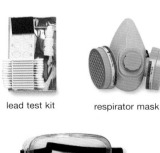

lead test kit

respirator mask

hard hat

goggles

ear defenders

work boots

Gaining easy access to all areas of a room is an important part of the safety at work code. Never risk injury by overstretching or overreaching – instead use ladders or access platforms so that you can reach all parts of a room with ease. This is especially the case for exterior work, where tower scaffolds or mechanical platforms may be a practical option. This kind of equipment can be hired and helps to provide a safe working environment, as well as saving time when extensive, high-level work is needed.

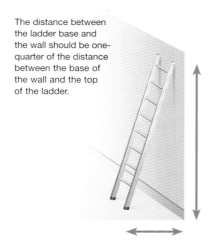

The distance between the ladder base and the wall should be one-quarter of the distance between the base of the wall and the top of the ladder.

Careful ladder positioning is vital for the safety of its user.

ladders

Ladders have always been the most commonly used and versatile of access equipment options. However, despite their simple construction and ease of use, there are a number of simple but important rules to obey when using them.

■ Ensure that the distance between the base of the ladder and the wall is one-quarter the distance between the base of the wall and top of the ladder.
■ Ensure that the ladder base is on a level, non-slip surface.
■ Ensure that the top of the ladder has total contact with the wall surface.
■ Ensure that all rungs are secure and have not been damaged in any way. The alternative to traditional ladders is to purchase multi-purpose versions that have many uses.

scaffold tower

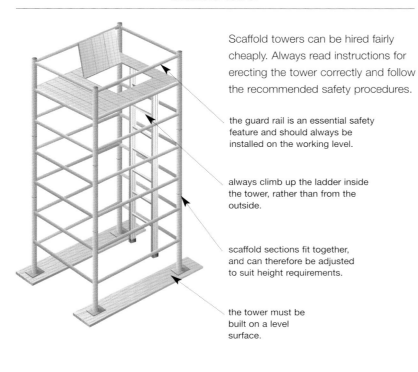

Scaffold towers can be hired fairly cheaply. Always read instructions for erecting the tower correctly and follow the recommended safety procedures.

the guard rail is an essential safety feature and should always be installed on the working level.

always climb up the ladder inside the tower, rather than from the outside.

scaffold sections fit together, and can therefore be adjusted to suit height requirements.

the tower must be built on a level surface.

GENERAL TOOL CARE

Accidents can often be caused by tools that have either been poorly maintained or are so old that they are no longer safe to use. Therefore careful tool maintenance will always ensure that you get the best out of your tools as well as making sure they are safe to use. Below are a few points to consider regarding maintenance and safety.

● Chisels, planes and cutting equipment must always be kept as sharp as possible. More accidents are caused by blunt tools slipping on the surface than by sharp tools. An oilstone is ideal to keep tools such as chisels razor sharp.

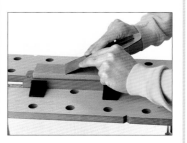

● Electric cables and wires on power tools can break or crack, so they should be inspected regularly to ensure they are in good condition. Power tools in general may also require periodic servicing. In addition, power tool efficiency can be hampered by the accessories you use with them. Therefore bits and blades should be renewed when necessary, as old ones can strain the workings of the power tool being used.

● Hammers can often slip right off the head of a nail when you are attempting to knock it in. To avoid this happening, sand the striking face of the hammer in order to both clean it and provide a fine key. It is surprising what a difference this simple procedure can make. This technique may be applied to all types of hammer and is useful for any hammering procedure.

inserting a doorway – 1 ⁄⁄⁄⁄

Inserting a doorway in a loadbearing wall is not a task that should be taken on lightly because of the structural nature of the work. As such, it is important to follow the correct procedures and techniques when tackling a project such as this. It is always advisable to seek some professional guidance before beginning work, as the procedure will vary slightly depending on the make-up of the wall and its exact position in the house structure as a whole.

The work involved is strongly based on supportive measures. This means supplying the necessary temporary support while the part of the wall for the doorway is removed, and supplying the necessary permanent support for above the doorway in the future. This latter point is crucial in that a lintel of some nature will be required to act as the permanent support. Its size and make-up will depend on two factors, namely the structure of the wall to be removed and the span of the proposed opening. Both of these require serious calculation, and the question of lintel type and construction should be decided in consultation with a structural engineer. Once all the necessary safety precautions and procedures are in place, and permission has been gained from a Building Control Officer, the actual work itself is eminently achievable. This can be divided into two stages: firstly, the opening has to be made and secondly, the lintel inserted.

making the opening

A methodical approach is required for this procedure and it is important to follow guidelines in the correct order. The work will produce a lot of dust and rubbish, so use dust sheets and arrange for the rubble and broken masonry to be disposed of.

1 Mark out the size of the opening on the wall surface.

2 Knock holes through the wall above the proposed opening.

3 Insert needles through the holes.

4 Support the needles by props on both sides of the wall.

5 Use a stone cutter or club hammer and bolster chisel to cut around the edge of the opening.

6 Remove the blocks or bricks by first loosening with a club hammer and bolster chisel and then levering them out with a wrecking bar or lift by hand.

7 Continue to remove blocks until the entire area is clear.

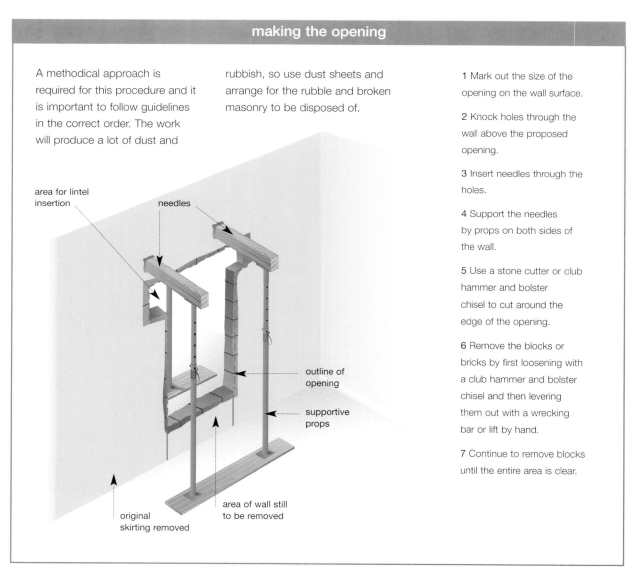

area for lintel insertion

needles

outline of opening

supportive props

original skirting removed

area of wall still to be removed

inserting the new lintel

It is essential for two people to be involved when inserting the lintel as they are surprisingly heavy. It is also much easier to carry out this procedure whilst working from some sort of access platform, rather than using stepladders.

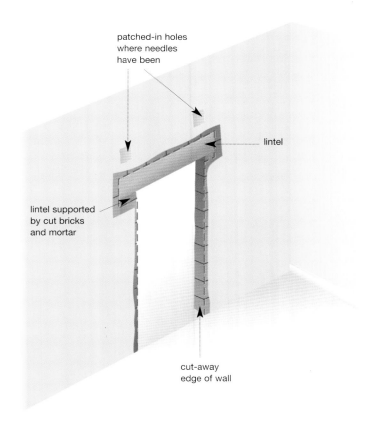

patched-in holes where needles have been

lintel

lintel supported by cut bricks and mortar

cut-away edge of wall

1 At the top corners of the opening take out bricks or blocks to accommodate the lintel ends.

2 Check and re-check measurements to ensure that the lintel will fit into the required space.

3 Apply a bed of mortar to this area before lifting the lintel into place.

4 Check that the lintel is level. Use cut bricks or blocks, wedged beneath the end of the lintel to rectify this if necessary.

5 Apply more mortar around the lintel ends to ensure it will be held securely in place.

6 Make good with plasterboard and/or render and plaster around the lintel.

7 Make good with plasterboard and/or render and plaster around the cut blocks or bricks that make up the sides of the opening.

8 Remove the needles and patch in the holes.

factors to consider

In addition to the practical considerations of how to support your wall, there are also a number of other issues that should be carefully addressed.

needle requirement

The number of needles required for support will depend on the width of the opening. Needle dimensions should not be less than 15cm x10cm (6in x 4in), but consult a structural engineer on exact requirements.

propping

Steel props can be hired at low cost and their adjustable nature makes them ideal for supporting purposes. Make sure that the bases of the props are positioned on scaffold planks so that weight distribution is evened out. Most prop bases have nail holes so that they can be nailed into the scaffold planks to eliminate any risk of them moving.

lintel support

In many cases the new lintel may be accommodated in the existing wall structure with no extra support below it required. However, in some cases it may be necessary to install extra concrete support. Consult a structural engineer for the correct requirements in your particular circumstances.

safety equipment

This sort of work requires close attention to safety and all the necessary precautions must be taken. Wear protective gloves, goggles and a hard hat when taking down the wall. A dust mask may also be needed, especially when clearing away the rubble and dust caused by wall removal.

inserting a doorway – 2

Inserting a doorway in a non-loadbearing wall is much easier than the technique used for a loadbearing wall. However, before work begins, you must be certain that the wall is non-loadbearing and it is always best to take professional advice to check this. For solid, block, non-loadbearing walls, a lintel is generally required and therefore the procedure is similar to that shown on pages 38–9. The example shown here deals with cutting an entrance into a non-loadbearing stud wall.

safety advice

As always, check that there are no services running through the stud wall, which will otherwise require re-routing before work can begin.

tools for the job

| joist detector |
| bradawl |
| pencil |
| spirit level |
| panel saw |
| tape measure |
| wrecking bar |
| cordless drill/driver |

1 Use a joist detector in order to locate the position of the vertical studs in the wall. It is essential that you locate a stud close to or directly where the hinged side of the door will eventually come to hang. Once the position of this stud has been located, all your other measurements should be taken from this point and will guide the process.

2 On the main stud, locate the exact edge of the timber by inserting a bradawl through the plasterboard at the detection points that you located by using the joist detector.

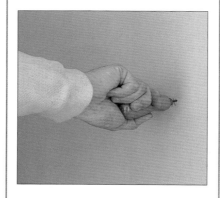

3 Join up the line of holes with a pencil and spirit level. A well-constructed stud wall should show this line to be exactly vertical. If this is not the case, the stud may require slight repositioning once exposed.

4 Measure out the rest of the entrance dimensions on the wall surface. For a standard internal door and doorway, remember to allow for the dimensions of the door plus the

thickness of the door lining, leaving an additional 6mm (¼in) to allow for a gap between door and frame. Remove the section of plasterboard by accurately sawing along the guidelines with a panel saw.

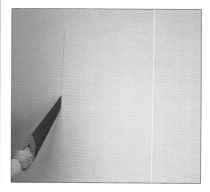

5 The other side of the wall will require cutting out as well. From 'inside' the wall, use a bradawl to pierce the plasterboard at the corners and positions corresponding to the initial opening. It is then possible to join these markings with a pencil on the other side of the wall, and again cut out the area with a panel saw. Remember to keep the edge of the saw tight against the stud.

6 Remove any vertical studs or noggings from the entrance with a panel saw, trimming back precisely to the plasterboard edge.

7 Cut away the sole plate with the panel saw, back to the edge of the plasterboard. If the sole plate is fixed in the entrance, it may be necessary to use a wrecking bar to prise it free. It is also recommended to add some fixings into the sole plate at the bottom corners of the 'entrance'. In this way, the cut sole plate will be secured firmly back in position.

8 Although the stud creating the hinging side of the entrance is precisely aligned with the edge of the plasterboard, it is unlikely that your measurements will have allowed the stud on the opposite door to align as accurately as possible. Therefore, it may be necessary to insert a vertical stud along this edge. Cut the timber to size and skew some screws in at the bottom of its length, which will make fixing easier and help you to secure the stud in place.

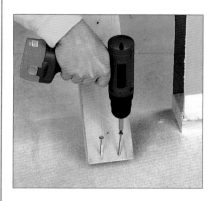

9 Skewing the screws in at an angle before the stud is positioned makes it easier to tighten the screws once it is in position. Depending on the wall structure it will then be necessary to fix the stud at the top of the entrance. Usually, there will be an existing wall nogging to help you. Alternatively, you may need to insert another nogging for secure fixing purposes.

10 Fill in the top part of the frame by cutting lengths of timber to the required size. Again skew screws into these lengths before tightening and driving them into position once the length is in place. Ensure that the screwheads enter into the wood so that they are below surface level.

11 Where vertical studs extend down to the top of the entrance, it is necessary to add further fixings to ensure rigidity. Fit a further length on the other side of the vertical length to finish off the entrance frame.

STUD WALL ISSUES

● **Dimensions** – Stud walls are generally constructed of timbers that are either 10cm x 5cm (4in x 2in) or 7.5cm x 5cm (3in x 2in) in dimension. Therefore before purchasing or re-using any wood to make the entrance, ensure that you know which stud dimensions will be required.

● **Use** – Entrances may be left open, doors inserted or other features such as arches added. When measuring for the entrance, calculating specific size requirements is vital, especially for doors, as sizes vary so much.

inserting a door lining ⚒⚒⚒

A door lining houses the hinges and closing mechanism, and provides the general perimeter for a door when 'positioned' in a wall surface. Linings tend to be supplied in a very simple kit form, and are then fitted to the precise aperture requirements. Although this is a very straightforward procedure, accuracy is essential as any deviation from totally vertical and square positioning will cause major problems when it comes to hanging a door.

tools for the job

wooden mallet
hammer
tape measure
pencil
panel saw
spirit level
cordless drill/driver

door linings

The sections that make up a lining are often referred to by different terms. For our purposes, the top part of the lining is called the 'head' and the side sections the 'stiles'.

1 Assemble the three parts of the lining on the floor. Put the stile ends into the pre-made slots in the head. They should fit relatively snugly but may need one or two blows with a mallet to ensure the joint is tight.

2 Secure the stiles in place by nailing through the top of the head into the stiles. Alternatively,

screw fixings may be used for this purpose. Ensure that each stile is secured with at least two fixings.

3 Measure the exact distance between the stiles at the head end of the lining. Transfer this measurement to the floor level of the lining and nail a length of batten between the stiles, securing them in position at this required width. Ensure that the batten does not extend past the outer edge of the lining, as this will hinder fitting the lining when it is positioned in the wall aperture.

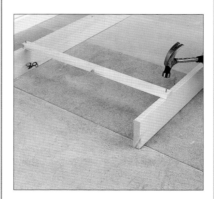

4 To ensure that the lining is totally 'square', it is necessary to make further measurements and fixings at

the top of the lining. Measuring away from the top corner of the lining, mark off one point at 30cm (12in) along the head, and another at 40cm (16in) along the stile. Adjust the distance between the 40cm (16in) mark and the 30cm (12in) mark on the head and ensure that it is exactly 50cm (20in). With these three measurements exact, this means that the lining itself is totally square.

5 Cut a length of batten to fit across the angle of the head and stile. Nail it in place, checking to ensure that the diagonal measurement of 50cm (20in) is maintained. The lining is now firmly braced at both the top and bottom.

6 Use a panel saw to cut off the excess head. Make sure that you cut right back to the corners of the lining, as leaving any excess will hinder its positioning in the wall.

7 Lift up the lining and position it in the wall opening. Concentrate on the 'hinged' side of the door. Use a spirit level to check that the lining is exactly vertical and the front edge is level with the wall surface on both sides.

8 Fix the 'hinging' side of the lining in place with screws, through the stile and into the timber below.

9 Depending on the precision of your measurements, it is likely that there will be a small gap between the stile and wall on the opposite side of the lining. Before trying to rectify this situation, make the fixing easier by starting off screws for fixing at intervals along the stile. Allow them to penetrate into the stile, but not through to the other side.

10 Cut some wooden wedges from offcuts and position them in the gap between the stile and wall. Position wedges at the screw fixing points. The best technique is to apply two wedges in each case, inserted from the opposite sides of the wall. In this way when the wedges meet, they can be gradually pushed in together to form a rigid support between the stile and wall.

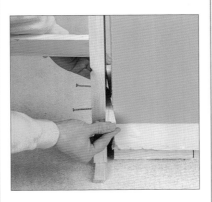

11 When all the wedges have been inserted, you can then secure the frame in place by continuing to insert the screw fixings, so that they go through the wedges and into the vertical stud of the wall.

Again, while you are inserting the screws continue to check the lining position with a spirit level.

12 Use a panel saw to cut off wedge excess as required (trim back flush). Add some final fixings to the head, screwing through into the horizontal stud above. Use wedges to pack out any spaces.

SOLID BLOCK WALLS

The technique for inserting door linings into solid block or brick walls is exactly the same as that shown here except that there will be a different fixings requirement. In order to deal with masonry, concrete anchor screws or frame fixings should be used for securing the lining in place.

● **The right lining** – Linings are sold in kit form and are thus, to a certain extent, standardized to correspond to modern wall and door dimensions. In older properties it may be necessary to make your own customized lining.

making an arch profile ⁊⁊⁊⁊

As well as fitting doors into wall openings, arch profiles can be used as an alternative to traditional doors or square openings, providing more of a feature between rooms. In the past it would have been a highly skilled procedure to produce a framework for an arch and finish it with subsequent coats of plaster. Today, however, manufacturing innovation has made the process much easier. Arch formers can be bought, positioned and plastered over to create perfect profiles.

making an arch profile in a stud wall

tools for the job

cordless drill/driver

screwdriver

hacksaw

hammer

tape measure

filling knife

plastering trowel

Although arch profiles may be built onto existing wall openings, beginning from scratch and building them into a new stud wall is by far the easiest procedure. A new wall, if erected correctly, is more likely to be true and square compared to older walls, thereby making the process of fitting the arch much more straightforward.

1 Most formers will have pre-drilled holes to accommodate fixings. Hold the former in position whilst drilling four pilot holes into the timber studs. Ensure that the front lip of the

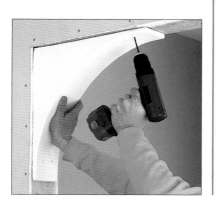

arch former corresponds to the manufacturer's guidelines in terms of encroaching up to the level of the plasterboard on either side of the wall.

2 Secure the former in place with wood screws. Use a screwdriver rather than a cordless drill/driver to tighten the screws, as overtightening could crack the plaster former. Greater control of movement can be achieved by using a simple hand tool in situations like this.

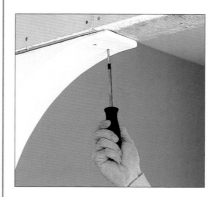

3 From the base of the arch former to the floor, it will be necessary to cut and fit plasterboard so as to cover the wooden stud and bring its surface up to the same

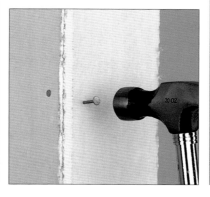

depth as the base of the arch former. Fix this strip in place with plasterboard nails in the usual manner taking care not to damage the plaster.

4 Cut angle bead to the correct length (former base to floor) and attach it on both edges of the opening. Fix it in position using plasterboard nails, ensuring that the apex of each angle bead aligns precisely with the respective bottom corners of the former.

5 Repeat steps 1–4 to fit the second former and entrance lining. It is rare that the dimensions of the formers will join exactly and therefore it is almost certain that there will be a gap between the top edges

👍 tips of the trade

Dry lined arches – An alternative technique to produce an arch profile. Instead of using angle bead along the vertical arch edges, corner tape can be applied and jointing compound used. The internal area of the former can also be filled with plaster bonding coat before being finished with jointing compound.

of the formers. Use the same technique as for the studs on each side of the entrance to fill the gap between the formers – in other words, fill the gap with plasterboard and use angle bead to form the edges.

6 Once the formers, plasterboard lining and angle beads have all been positioned and aligned, fill the arch former holes with all-purpose filler or bonding coat plaster.

7 Tape the plasterboard joints with self-adhesive jointing tape, and also the joints between the plasterboard and the arch formers.

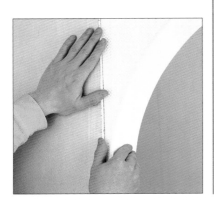

8 Apply plaster to the walls, making sure that you extend the plaster over and onto the arched formers. The actual arched face of the formers may not require plastering depending on the type of former you have used. Once the plaster has been 'polished' and dries, the arch is ready for decoration. With some formers, it may be necessary to apply two coats of plaster.

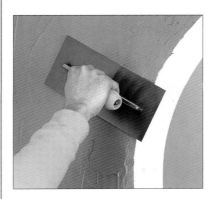

tips of the trade

● **Blending** – Where the smooth former face meets the plastered edge of the entrance, it may be necessary to 'feather' the join with fine filler in order to provide a perfectly smooth arched profile. Once filled, use a fine grade sandpaper to finish the join.

● **Dealing with cracks** – In most cases, as long as the formers have been securely positioned and the arch has been plastered correctly, joint cracks are unlikely to appear. However, if cracks do appear, and are not lost by refilling and painting, it is worth lining the arch with lining paper, thus covering any hairline cracks should they try to reappear in the plaster surface itself. This technique will only cover small cracks and anything larger suggests the arch profile has not been fitted correctly, in which case it may be necessary to begin the fitting procedure from the beginning again.

Arches add shape to rooms and soften edges, producing a relaxed and comfortable atmosphere. They also help to link decoration between two living areas.

closing up a doorway – 1 ⤨

When a doorway needs to be blocked up, the first consideration is whether the wall itself is of a solid block or brick construction, or is composed of a stud framework. If the former is the case, it is always best to close up the opening using blocks or bricks, as the dimensions of the materials you use will be more suitable than stud work, and employing similar materials to those used in the construction of the rest of the wall will generally make the project far easier to carry out.

tools for the job

wrecking bar
cordless drill/driver
screwdriver
hammer
trowel
spirit level
plastering trowel

1 The first task is to remove the door and frame from the entrance. The door may simply be unscrewed from its hinges, but the frame, or the door lining, will almost certainly require levering free from surrounding blockwork. A wrecking bar is the ideal tool for this purpose and should be able to prise the lining away and remove any fixings.

2 The blocks which are inserted will require some form of tying in to the existing wall for strength and stability. There are a number of different frame tie designs, and the types used here require screwing into the blocks in the entrance. Drill a series of holes for the plugs at the

mortar levels, so that the ties will be inserted at the same level for tying into the new mortar between the blocks used in the entrance.

3 Insert the plastic wall plug into the drilled hole and screw in the wall tie tight up to the collar. You may need to use some sort of lever mechanism to make the last few turns of the tie. Holding a screwdriver across and between the V-shape of the tie design, and using it to rotate and lever the tie into position, should produce a firm fixing.

4 Mix up and apply a bed of mortar along the floor between the two sides of the entrance.

The mortar should be laid at about the width of a block and be generous enough to provide a good bedding for block placement.

5 Butter the end of the first block with mortar, giving it a good 'cone'-shaped coverage. Be fairly generous with the mortar, without applying too much of an excess so that it keeps falling off and away from the top of the block. Use a gauging trowel for this purpose, smoothing around the edge of the block to form good adhesion between the mortar and the block. This is also a good test to see if your mortar mix is of the correct consistency. It should hold a firm but pliable shape on top of the block.

1 Remove door, door lining and architrave.

2 Build up blocks in aperture, using frame ties to tie them in with the surrounding blockwork or by removing blocks at alternate levels on either side of the aperture so that new blocks are tied in with the existing wall structure.

3 Fill area between the top level of blocks and the lintel with bricks.

4 Render blocks or apply plaster scratch coat.

5 Apply final plaster skim to render.

6 Fill in with missing section of skirting or replace entire section of skirting along length of wall.

7 Sand new plastered area and decorate as required.

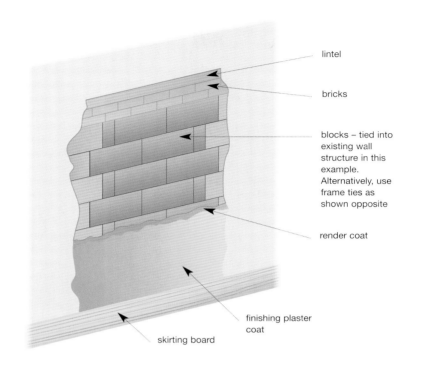

lintel

bricks

blocks – tied into existing wall structure in this example. Alternatively, use frame ties as shown opposite

render coat

finishing plaster coat

skirting board

6 Position the block on the bed of mortar under the first frame tie, forcing the buttered end of the block tight up against the entrance surface. Use a spirit level to ensure the block is correctly positioned. Continue to build up levels until the entrance is filled. Remember to insert frame ties at each level to ensure that the new blockwork forms a strong bond with the existing wall. Also make sure that the vertical joints between successive levels of blockwork are staggered.

FURTHER POINTS TO NOTE

• Frame tie alternatives
Instead of using frame ties, it is just as effective to remove the first block on every other course, and in this way create a staggered effect allowing the new blocks to be tied into the old wall.

• Cutting blocks
Concrete blocks may either be cut with a stone cutter, which you will probably have to hire, or using a club hammer and bolster chisel. For either method, be sure to wear goggles for safety reasons.

• Wooden floors
When closing up an opening on a wooden floor, you will need to insert a wooden sole plate across the bottom of the entrance, which will help to provide a more rigid base, and build up your blockwork on top of this. Otherwise, the flexibility of a wooden floor may fracture the joints in the blockwork as you progress.

• Neat joints
Although the blockwork will be covered with both render and plaster, it is still important to make the joints between the blocks as neat as possible. Smooth, finished joints will be much easier to render over than if you leave any rough mortar edges between blocks. Therefore, after each block has been positioned, be sure to use a trowel to remove excess mortar from the face of the joints before it dries out.

• Improving the finish
However proficient your blockwork and plastering skills are, making a blocked-up entrance in a wall completely 'disappear' after redecoration is a difficult task. Make sure that after plastering you undertake some fine filling and sanding along the join between the new and old walls. You might also want to consider lining the wall before painting, as this will again make any joins less noticeable.

closing up a doorway – 2

When closing up a doorway in a stud wall, the work involved becomes a case of filling in the wood and plasterboard framework to provide as flat a finish as possible. One of the most important considerations is to ensure that the studs and plasterboard you use are of similar dimensions to the actual wall. Different stud walls have varying depths depending on the house and its particular age. Do not therefore make the mistake of purchasing the wrong materials before you begin.

tools for the job

screwdriver

wrecking bar

panel saw

cordless drill/driver

hammer

craft knife

straight edge or spirit level

scraper

plastering float

tips of the trade

Remember that when you fill in or close up an old entrance, it is likely that services will need re-routing. For example, light switches – which are normally found close to an entrance – will look out of place once the opening has been closed up. You should therefore make the appropriate arrangements, before starting off the closing up project, to have switches moved and any other services whose position may require some adjustment.

1 Unscrew the door from its hinges and remove it from the opening. Use a wrecking bar to lever the architrave away from the wall surface. Take care not to allow the wrecking bar to dig into and damage the existing wall surface.

2 Once again use the wrecking bar to lever the door lining away from the studs. The ease with which this comes away will depend upon whether the lining wad is fixed in position with nails or screws. If nails have been used, lining removal tends to be much easier.

3 Fill in the missing section of sole plate by cutting a piece of timber to length and fitting it at the base of the entrance. Pilot hole and screw it securely in position.

4 Cut a vertical length of timber to the height of the frame and secure it in position, again with screws. Add another length on the other side of the frame, and then a central stud running from the middle of the new section of sole plate up to the centre of the stud which was above the door frame.

5 Add extra rigidity to the three new vertical studs by fitting noggings between each one. Skew screws through the noggins and into the vertical studs in order to provide extra strength of fixing. Nails may also be used for this purpose as long as they hold the noggings very securely in position.

6. Rather than using a large plasterboard sheet, which would require accurate cutting to fit into the framework aperture, use smaller laths fitted horizontally. These are easier to handle and trim to size. Hold a lath in position at the top of the aperture and accurately mark off the cutting requirement using a pencil.

7. Lie the lath flat on the floor and use a craft knife to score a line in the plasterboard between the pencil guidelines. A spirit level provides an excellent straight edge to guide the blade of the craft knife. Once scored, turn the lath over and snap it upwards to break it along the scored line.

8. Place the cut lath back in the aperture and carefully nail it into position. Continue to measure and fit more laths until the aperture is filled. Carry out the same procedure on the other side of the wall – you may wish to fill the void with insulation blanket before this second part of the plasterboarding process. If you do choose to insulate the wall, remember to wear protective gloves as the insulation fibres may otherwise cause skin irritation.

9. Apply self-adhesive jointing tape along all the joins, both between the plasterboard laths and the existing wall, and along the join between each lath. Smooth the tape to ensure there are no lumps or wrinkles in its surface.

10. You now have the choice of dry lining or plastering the plasterboard. Dry lining should only be considered an option if the new plasterboard level is flush with that of the existing wall. Otherwise, the old entrance will appear slightly recessed into the wall surface once decorated. Plastering the whole area is thus normally a more suitable option. Before applying a skim, fill along all the taped joints with some bonding plaster to provide a good base for the plaster. Once this has dried, apply a skim of finishing plaster to the whole area, feathering a join with the existing wall surface. Repeat this procedure on the other side of the wall. Once all the plaster has dried, the missing skirting board can be filled in and the walls decorated.

PREPARING TO DECORATE

To achieve a good finish and make the 'closing' as unnoticeable as possible, there are a few final procedures that will improve its 'invisible' effect.

● **Fine sanding** – Although a standard procedure for preparation, sanding is even more vital when trying to blend in an old doorway. The application of some fine filler, followed by further sanding, will improve the smooth nature of the final finish.

● **Closed doorway painting** – When painting a stud wall, even if you are using an identical colour to that of the rest of the wall, the old doorway will invariably still show up. It is therefore best to prime the newly plastered area, apply a first coat of finishing paint and then apply the top coat over the entire stud wall. This may sound extravagant, but it does tend to make such old doorways less noticeable in the overall finish.

● **Lining** – The best option is to line the entire wall after the old doorway has been closed up. The thickness of the lining paper (1000–1200 microns is ideal) helps to smooth the wall surface further and reduces the likelihood of the closed-up area remaining apparent. Once lined, all the walls may be painted.

fitting doors

Fitting a door requires a methodical technique that can be adapted to take into account variations in door design and function. The actual principle and method remains similar with all doors but it can be necessary to make variations during installation depending on such factors as whether the door is internal or external and what type of hinges are being used. This chapter looks at many of these variations in door design and use, and demonstrates the most common procedures for fitting not only the door but all the accessories required for its correct functioning. This includes such items as the handles needed for opening and closing, and the relevant security fittings that have become an essential requirement in modern everyday life. Doors are crucial components in how your home functions and therefore close attention to detail will ultimately be rewarding.

Picked up in a salvage yard, this door was trimmed to size and given a makeover with etched-glass panelling.

choosing options

Door choice may initially be broken down into two categories – whether the door is internal or external. After this, choice becomes a combination of personal style preference and price considerations. Depending upon the quality of the product there is a huge variation in door price. Attention should be directed to how the door has been made, and its general quality in terms of the materials it has been made with, before making a final decision on a specific style.

external doors

Owing to the fact that external doors are exposed to the elements, their manufacture and make up tends to be more hardwearing than interior equivalents. They may also be slightly wider and thicker in depth than internal doors.

hardwood panel

Standard, good quality choice of external door. Hardwood provides excellent protection from weathering.

pvc

Usually fitted to match pvc windows. A very hardwearing option because of its resistance to weathering.

stable

Traditional style of door that divides into two separate opening sections. Requires four hinges.

hardwood part glazed

Decorative option to a solid panel hardwood door. Glazing allows for more light to flow into darker hallways.

glazed

Totally glazed external doors improve further the amount of light that can be brought into an entrance hall.

exterior frame

The exterior frame of a door is a vital part of its functioning success. Quality is again vital, with a hardwood threshold an excellent option.

Internal doors are generally narrower than external ones and not as thick or as deep. Designs and styles tend to be more varied since there is less need in the door's design to take into account their weathering capabilities.

solid softwood panel

Common choice of internal door offering attractive but simple, traditional design features.

softwood glazed

Excellent for allowing light into rooms and through dark hallways. Glazing does add considerable cost.

pressed panel

Pressed panel doors are an option to solid ones and are often considerably cheaper than solid equivalents.

flush

Economical choice of door that has a totally flat face. A good choice for people constrained by a tight budget.

louvre

Generally used for cupboard doors rather than entrances. Lightweight and not the most hardwearing.

ledge and brace

Traditional-looking door of which more substantial varieties are often used as external doors.

external view   internal view

wooden doors

The main issue with buying wooden doors is ensuring that the wood will not warp in the future and therefore cause problems in terms of opening and shutting. Much of this concern can be dealt with by spending a little extra to buy good quality, and also by sealing the surface of the door immediately it is hung to avoid moisture penetration.

modern innovation

Along with pvc doors, other modern materials are now used in door construction. Steel or fibreglass, for example, are commonly being used to face doors, especially external ones. The idea is again to increase hardwearing properties, reduce the risk of the door warping or going out of shape, and increase security options.

door furniture & security fittings

Doors clearly need the appropriate fixtures and fittings in order that they can function properly. Although this is a mainly practical concern, there is considerable choice in terms of style and design when it comes to purchasing door furniture. Add to this the relevant security features that may be needed and the options expand further. It is, therefore, necessary to look at some examples of what is available so that you can make the right choices for your particular needs.

handles

Door handles can broadly be placed into two categories – those that have a basic knob design and those that operate in a lever fashion. Nearly all operate the closing and opening mechanism of a door, the latch, by means of a spindle joining the two handles on a door through the latch mechanism. On doors that do not have a latch mechanism, such as cupboard doors which may use a simple spring-loaded ball catch, a spindle is not required and the handles merely act as a secure gripping point to open the door. Shown on the right are some examples of common door handles and the latch sets they may operate in conjunction with. Owing to the fact that there are many different designs available it is possible to combine their style with the relevant security features which may also be used on the door.

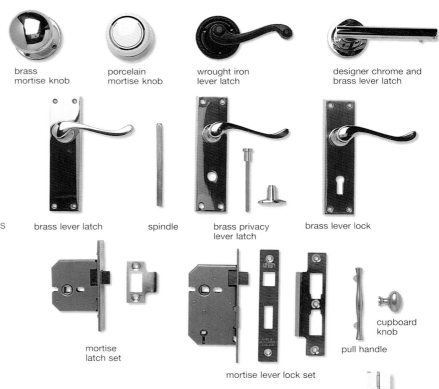

brass mortise knob

porcelain mortise knob

wrought iron lever latch

designer chrome and brass lever latch

brass lever latch

spindle

brass privacy lever latch

brass lever lock

mortise latch set

mortise lever lock set

pull handle

cupboard knob

hinges

Straightforward butt hinges are used as the hinging mechanism on most entrance and cupboard doors in the home. Even though most of the hinge is concealed when the door is shut, there are still some designs that display decorative appeal. Exposed hinges, such as the antique iron one shown, are used most commonly in conjunction with traditional door designs such as a stable door or ledge and brace. Piano hinges are also an option for cupboard doors.

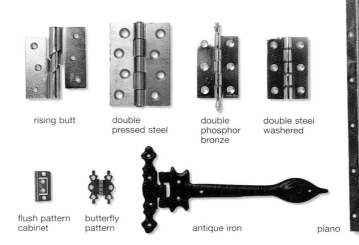

rising butt

double pressed steel

double phosphor bronze

double steel washered

flush pattern cabinet

butterfly pattern

antique iron

piano

Door security features are mainly concerned with external doors, although some items are used in conjunction with rooms of privacy such as bathrooms. Most devices either interact directly with the handle latch mechanism, or are separate to this and used as extra security devices on other areas of the door. Since security is such an important issue in modern society, system designs vary considerably. On the right are examples of the security mechanisms available, catering for many different requirements.

tips of the trade

It is worth remembering that although good security products can be expensive, this expense can usually be offset against peace of mind and the possibility of lower insurance premiums. Higher prices do also tend to guarantee that the product will be long-lasting and function correctly throughout its working life.

door viewer with cover

door viewer

cylinder pull

door limiter

security chain

knob side flush bolt

door bolt

mortise door bolt

cylinder rim lock

slim-style rim lock

lever dead lock

Aside from the essential opening, closing and security aspects of door furniture, there are other items that can be applied to a wide range of door surfaces, either to complement those already mentioned or to fulfil another specific function. Fire doors, for example, will definitely require door closers. Most of these items have a highly decorative aspect to their make-up and so need to be chosen with this aesthetic requirement in mind. All these features are generally less complicated to fit compared to other door furniture. It is therefore worthwhile making these additions to improve the look and give some excess function to the door as a whole.

letter plate

concealed door closer

door knocker

finger plate

brass escutcheon

brass door closer

brass covered escutcheon

porcelain escutcheon

skirting door stop

door furniture & security fittings

55

cutting to size ✂✂✂

It is unlikely that a door will fit perfectly into the door lining or frame and so some cutting to size will probably be required, though trimming a door too much may weaken its structure. This is particularly true of 'hollow' doors that are based on a simple wooden frame. Most doors can be cut down using saws and planes, but for proprietary doors that are steel faced, or made of fibreglass or carbon fibre, the manufacturer's guidelines for fitting should be observed.

internal panel door

Fitting a solid panel door provides an ideal demonstration of the best technique for cutting a door to size. If you have fitted a new lining, then trimming the door to size should be straightforward. Fitting a new door to an old lining can be more complicated, but the same basic technique can be followed in both cases. Firstly, the door must be trimmed to less than the size of the aperture. Once this is achieved, precise fitting can be carried out.

tools for the job

hammer

pencil

tape measure

spirit level or straightedge

wood plane or power plane

board or door lifter

1 Insert two nails into the head of the lining. Their distance from the front of the head should be equal

to the depth of the door. In this way, when the door is placed in position in the lining, it will not fall through and will be supported securely enough to carry out the fitting procedure.

2 Fit the door in the lining, and mark off around the edge of the door to provide a 3mm (⅛in) clearance between the two vertical door stiles and the lining stiles. Depending on the 'squareness' of the lining, this may require more wood to be trimmed in some areas than in others.

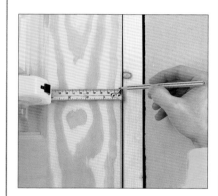

POWER PLANES

A power plane is an excellent tool for trimming down doors quickly and are especially useful when there is more than just a few millimetres to be shaved off.

tips of the trade

Excess trimming – Where the amount of wood to be shaved off a door edge is more than can be done with a plane, it may be necessary to use a jigsaw with a fine cutting blade.

3 Join up the marked-off points along the door edge using a straightedge or spirit level.

4 It may also be necessary to trim the height of the door, depending on whether the lining is square, and/or if the floor is level. Adjust your measurements to account for the required floor clearance.

5 Use a pencil to join markings, so that a precise guideline for trimming purposes is achieved.

6 Plane along the edge of the door to remove wood down as far as the pencil guideline. Clamp the door in a workbench for this procedure as this will hold it steady during the planing process.

7 Plane along the leading edge of the door at a slight angle, so that a little more wood is being taken off the edge, which will eventually be the closing edge of the door. This fractional extra wood removal will

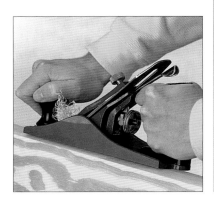

make the door clearance slightly larger on the back of the leading edge than on the front. This makes the clearance between door and lining much more even and reduces the risk of the door sticking in the future.

8 Once the door edges have been trimmed to fit and are checked in the entrance for size, trim down the top and/or bottom of the door as required. A plane may also be used for this process. Since this will mean working the plane over the end grain of the vertical stiles, only work the plane in a direction into the door and not towards its edge, which may cause the grain to split and damage the look of it.

9 A board or door lifter is the ideal tool to hold the door in place whilst clearances and preciseness of fit are measured. It also allows you to support the weight of the door, lifting or lowering it into the desired position. It is best to position the door lifter below the central stile and bottom rail.

10 Wedge the door in place at the top and bottom, butting it up tightly against what will be the hinged side. Measure the distance between the leading edge and the door lining to check that it is exactly 6mm (¼in), which will allow for a clearance of 3mm (⅛in) on both edges of the door once it is accurately hung in position.

EXTERIOR DOORS

The fitting process for an external door is very similar to that for an interior, except that an external door will always be fitted into a frame rather than into a lining. Apart from this, the same principles of cutting to size are employed. It is also likely that you will need to cut a rebate into the bottom of the door in order to accommodate the weather bar on the door sill. This can be achieved using a router. Some doors will come with 'horns' extending from the ends of the vertical stiles. This elongation of the stiles is simply a measure to protect the end grain before fitting. Accordingly, they should be cut off prior to the fitting process.

Exterior doors are generally much more expensive than interior doors, mainly because they are built to fulfil a more hardwearing requirement than their interior counterparts. Mistakes may therefore be costly, and so it is wise to take extra time in your measuring process, ensuring that you do not waste any materials.

cutting in hinges ✐✐✐

The accuracy of cutting in hinges is the vital factor that ensures the ease and efficiency with which a door opens and closes. External doors should always have three hinges because they tend to be heavier than internal ones. Three hinges also lessen the chances of a new door going out of shape and are therefore a good option if you have purchased relatively cheap doors. However, most internal doors may be hung successfully using two standard butt hinges.

tools for the job

tape measure
combination square
wooden mallet
chisel
cordless drill/driver
door lifter

1 Mark the hinge positions on the door edge, 15cm (6in) from the top of the door and 22.5cm (9in) up from the bottom of the door.

2 At the top marking, position the hinge wrong side up and directly below the 15cm (6in)

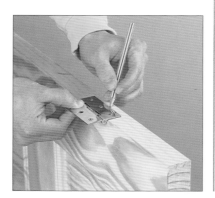

measurement. Holding it wrong side up allows the hinge barrel to be held flush against the door edge, which will ensure that the hinge position is marked off in the correct place. Draw a guideline around the edge of the hinge.

3 To measure the depth of the hinges you are using, hold one against a combination square. Adjust the ruler on the square to the depth of the hinge and lock it in position.

4 Hold the combination square perpendicular to the door edge so that the depth measurement for the hinge may be drawn accurately on the face of the door.

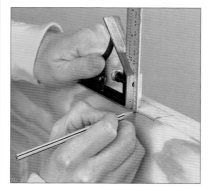

5 Use a wooden mallet and sharp chisel to remove the wood to the marked-off depth by making chisel indentations for the top and bottom edge of the hinge. This prevents the wood splitting when you chisel a guideline along the vertical length of the hinge marking.

6 The wood needs to be removed gradually to ensure accuracy and depth of the cut. Make a number of chisel cuts horizontally along where the hinge position will be, allowing the chisel to penetrate only as far as the depth measurement on the face of the door. Knocking the chisel in too far will cause an uneven surface once the recess wood is removed.

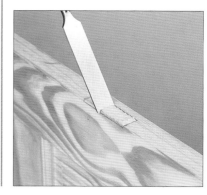

7 Now position the chisel so that its blade can be inserted beneath and at right angles to the horizontal cuts. Carefully lever up and remove the wooden sections, taking care not to allow the chisel to extend over the hinge guidelines.

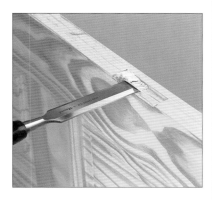

8 Repeat steps 2–7 at the base of the door for the bottom hinge, but hold the hinge above the 22.5cm (9in) measurement.
Then put the door in position in the door lining and place an open hinge between the top of the door and the door lining. This gives the measurement for the door clearance at the top and so allows you to mark off the hinge positions accurately on the door lining. Mark off at the top and bottom of the hinge position for both the top and bottom hinge.

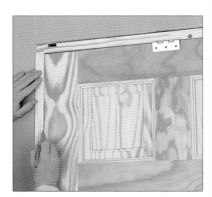

9 Remove the door and – in a similar way to marking off on the door edge – again hold a hinge wrong side up on the door lining and mark around it with a sharp pencil. Measure hinge depth and chisel out as required

in the same manner as used for the door edge. Carry out this process for both the top and bottom hinge.

10 Hold a hinge, right side up and in position, on the door edge. Make pencil marks for the screw positions, allowing the pencil point to move fractionally away from the screw hole centre and towards the back edge of the hinge.

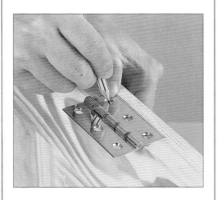

11 Remove the hinge and drill pilot holes for the screws. Be as accurate as possible, ensuring that the drill bit is inserted directly at the marked-off pencil points.

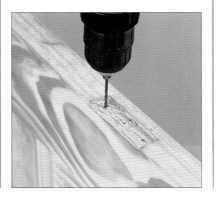

tips of the trade

Rising butts – Instead of fitting standard butt hinges, it may sometimes be necessary to fit rising butts. These lift the level of the door as it is opened. Cutting in rising butt hinges is similar to standard butt hinges but ensure you have right- or left-handed hinges, to suit the way the door opens. Also, bevel the top corner edge of the door (nearest to the hinges) so that it will be able to shut properly.

12 Reposition the hinge and insert screws into the pilot holes. Do not tighten the screws until all three are in place and the hinge is in the correct position. Repeat steps 10–12 for the bottom hinge.

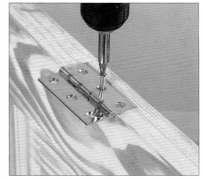

13 Hold the door open but in position in the door lining. Ensure that each hinge fits exactly into the chiselled-out positions. Mark with a pencil and pilot drill, before screwing the hinges in place. The door should open and close into the lining with a perfectly smooth action.

fitting handles – 1 ↗

Handles are fitted in three stages, which relate to the main components required for handles to work. Firstly, it is necessary to fit the latch; secondly, the handles themselves; and, thirdly, the strike plate has to be fitted in the door lining. Although, in the following example, a mortice lever lock has been used, the fitting principals are the same as for a simple mortise latch.

fitting the latch

1 Hold the latch on one face of the door at the required height. Allow the latch plate to overlap onto the edge of the door, so that the main latch casing sits flush against the door surface. Make a pencil mark along the top of the latch, one at the bottom, and two at the sides to show the height of the spindle position and the height of the keyhole.

2 Using a combination square, make horizontal guidelines to the marked-off points on the door face. Ensure that the combination square is held tight against the edge of the door so that the guidelines are accurate. Continue these lines onto the edge of the door and round to the other face, thus making a mirror image of the guidelines.

3 Measure the exact width of the door edge and lock the combination square to half this measurement. Use it to draw a central guideline vertically through the horizontal guidelines on the door edge.

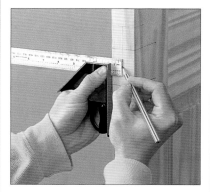

4 Use the combination square again to measure the distance between the front of the latch plate and the centre of the spindle hole. Lock the square in position at the correct measurement. You may allow a fraction extra to this measurement in order to compensate for the depth of the latch plate as it will be recessed into the door edge.

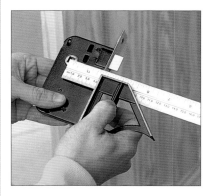

5 Transfer this measurement to the door edge, lining up the square with the pencil guideline, which denotes the spindle height on the door face. Make a vertical line through the horizontal one to provide a pin-point cross. Repeat this on the other side of the door. Repeat steps 4 and 5 to mark the exact position of the keyhole on the appropriate horizontal guidelines on the door. Double-check both measurements as mistakes are difficult to rectify later.

tips of the trade

Accuracy is key when fitting latches, so it is essential that the chisels you are using are razor sharp. Therefore, before you start fitting the handles, make sure that you have serviced these tools as it will certainly help to ensure that the job is completed to a high standard. See also the General Tool Care section on page 37.

6 Use an auger or flat drill bit to bore into the edge of the door along the vertical pencil guideline. The size of the bit should correspond to the width of the latch casing, not the width of the latch plate. Measure the depth of the latch and transfer this length to the drill bit, marking it with a piece of insulation tape. This way, it is possible to drill accurately to the required latch depth. Work down the vertical guideline, making a series of overlapping drilled holes. Ensure that the drill bit enters the door edge at right angles to the door so that the depth of holes remains consistent.

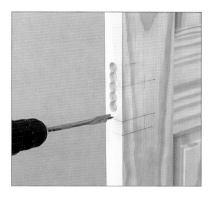

7 At the marked-off crosses for the spindle and keyhole, drill through the door using the correct size of auger or flat bit. It may be necessary to drill two overlapping holes to accommodate the keyhole. To avoid splitting the wood, drill from the marked-off points on both sides of the door, as drilling all the way through from one side can cause damage to the face of the door when the bit breaks through the surface.

8 Use a chisel to straighten the edges of the overlapping drilled holes along the door edge. Work methodically to produce clean and accurate cuts. Make safety cuts horizontally against the grain at the top and bottom of the hole. This will prevent the splitting of the wood.

9 Push the latch into the hole and carefully draw a precise pencil guideline around the latch plate on the edge of the door. There is little room for error at this stage and therefore take time to ensure that the latch is perfectly vertical, with the spindle and keyhole exactly aligned, before marking off.

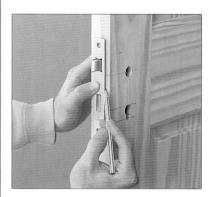

10 Take out the latch and chisel around the guideline, removing a depth of wood equal to that of the depth of the latch plate. Take care not to split the wood, by again using safety cuts to slice across the grain at the top and bottom horizontal guideline, before making cuts along the vertical guideline, and therefore along the grain of the wood.

Carefully remove the loosened wood until the correct level has been achieved and the plate sits flush.

11 Reposition the latch, allowing the chiselled-out area to accommodate the latch plate. The plate should be vertical and sit flush with the door edge. Drill pilot holes for the screws.

12 Finally, screw the latch in place, securing it in position with screws at top and bottom of the plate. Ensure the screws are done up well, but do not overtighten and risk distorting the face of the latch plate.

fitting handles – 2 ⚒

With the latch in position, the next step is to fit the handles to the door. Most handles are made to fit on a standard spindle, which in turn is inserted through the door and latch. This allows you to choose handles according to your own personal tastes. In this case a lever lock handle has been used to demonstrate the general technique required for fitting purposes.

tools for the job

bradawl

cordless drill/driver

screwdriver

tape measure

pencil

combination square

chisel

fitting the handles to the door

1 Initially, position the spindle through the door and latch, to check that it fits precisely. If the position is slightly off, the spindle movement may be hindered and therefore it is essential to check that its positioning is free from obstruction of any kind.

2 Fit one handle onto the spindle and hold it in the correct position, vertical to the door surface. This can be checked with a torpedo level, but it is usually possible to check its position by eye by judging the distance at the top and bottom of the handle plate relative to the door edge. Use a bradawl to make marks or indentations on the door surface through the handle plate screw holes.

3 Remove the handle and use a small drill bit to create pilot holes in the marks. Do not penetrate the surface much, as the holes are just a starting point for the screw insertion.

4 Reposition the handle and carefully screw it in place. It is best to insert the screws in a particular order to ensure that the handle stays level. Start at the top, inserting a screw in one corner and then fix the second screw in the opposite diagonal corner at the bottom of the handle plate. Finish with the other top screw followed by the final bottom one. This makes it easier to ensure that the handle is precisely aligned throughout the process of screw insertion.

THE OTHER SIDE

Repeat steps 2–4 on the other side of the door to fix the other handle in place. If, when you first position this handle, the length of the spindle prevents the handle plate from sitting flush against the door surface, it will be necessary to remove the spindle and cut it down to size. Spindles are supplied as multi-purpose items to fit all depths of door, so it is often the case that spindle cutting will be required. This is a simple process, which can be achieved with the use of a standard hacksaw. Once trimmed down, reposition the spindle and fit the handle.

👍 tips of the trade

When screwing handles in place, it is always best to use a hand held screwdriver, rather than a power driver. You have greater control to ensure that the handle is positioned vertically and there is less chance that the screwdriver head can slip and scratch the surface of the brass. Such scratches are irreparable.

fitting the strike plate

Once the latch and handle are fitted, attention can be turned to the catch mechanism, or strike plate, which requires fitting to the door lining.

1 In a locked position, close the door onto the door lining, allowing the latch and lock to rest against the lining. Then make pencil marks on the lining edge to denote the top and bottom positions of the latch and lock. Make these guidelines as clearly as possible for accuracy is very important.

2 Open the door and continue the marked-off pencil lines on the lining edge, around and onto the face of the door lining.

3 Holding the door in an open position, it is now necessary to measure the precise depth of the latch and the lock and along the door edge in order to gauge the correct position of the strike plate. Lock the

combination square at this depth measurement by tightening the ruler retaining screw.

4 Transfer the depth measurement, making a vertical guideline for the front of the latch and the lock respectively, between the appropriate horizontal lining guidelines.

5 Hold the strike plate in position. Mark around the strike plate to give its exact position requirement.

6 Chisel out inside the latch and lock guidelines and the external guideline for the strike plate. Position the strike plate, drill pilot holes and then screw it in place.

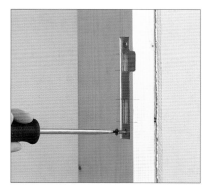

Once door furniture is fitted and the doorstop and architrave are fixed in place, the entire area may be decorated to reveal an attractive finished product.

finishing the frame ⤢

A door should be finished off with a doorstop and architrave. The doorstop prevents the door from closing further than flush with the wall surface. Failure to fit one will mean the door can be closed too far and you will risk damaging the hinges. The architrave, however, fulfils a purely decorative role, adding a finish to the lining and an overall frame to the door.

tools for the job

panel saw

hammer

pencil

torpedo level

mitresaw or mitre block

tape measure

nail punch

external doors

Most external doors do not require a doorstop to be fitted as there is one already built into the frame. Similarly, the exterior of the frame does not need an architrave, but the interior can be surrounded with one if required.

fitting the doorstop

Doorstops vary in dimension, but are normally about 3.75cm x 1cm (1½in x ⅜in) in cross section. Sizes vary according to the door dimensions and between manufacturers. Normally a doorstop is supplied as part of the door lining kit.

1 Close the door so that you are on the inside side of the door lining. Carefully draw a pencil guideline on the lining at the position where the door meets the lining. Open the door, and cut lengths of doorstop to fit the head of the lining and down the two stiles. Start by positioning the doorstop at the head

of the lining. Check that it fits precisely before proceeding to fix it in position. Use wire nails for fixing.

2 Nail the head doorstop in place so that its front edge aligns precisely with the pencil guideline. Do not knock the nails all the way in at this stage – simply insert them far enough to be secure, but so that the nail head is still protruding. This allows removal and repositioning to be achieved easily, if it is necessary.

3 Cut and fit the length of doorstop on the strike plate stile. Then cut and fit the doorstop on the hinge side of the lining. Instead of

positioning this length along the pencil line, fix it slightly back from the line. This deviation will allow the hinge edge to shut easily and prevent it catching on the doorstop. Finish off by knocking the nails right in after opening and closing the door to check the action.

fitting the architrave

Once you have chosen the architrave style, fitting is relatively simple as long as cuts are accurate and a mitresaw or mitre block is used during this process. Remember that, for the best decorative effect, the architrave should be chosen to match with the other mouldings in the room such as the skirting board and dado or picture rails, if appropriate.

1 Use an offcut of the architrave to determine corner positions. Hold the piece in place above the door, approximately 0.5cm (³⁄₁₆in) to 1cm (⅜in) away from the lining edge. This distance is often decided by aesthetic preference and is a matter of personal

choice. However, once you have chosen it, you must ensure that it remains consistent around the entire door lining. Draw a pencil guideline along the top of the architrave, which extends out onto the wall surface to the side of the door, as this will help you to maintain consistency.

2 Hold the offcut vertically along the hinged side of the lining, keeping the same distance between the architrave edge and the door lining edge as per the distance that was employed at the top of the door. If you draw another pencil guideline along the outer edge of the architrave, it will then cross over the horizontal pencil guideline. Next, repeat steps 1 and 2 at the other corner of the lining. These pencil lines will now provide you with the precise guidelines for what will be the outside corners of your architrave.

3 Measure the length requirement for the top section of architrave by measuring between the two points where the pencil guidelines cross

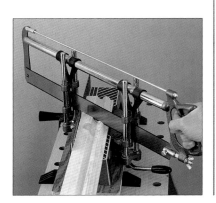

above each corner of the door. Mark off this distance along the back edge of a piece of architrave. Then use a mitresaw to cut your architrave accurately to size.

4 Position the architrave above the door lining and nail it in position. Ideally, attach the length so that the nails protrude into the edge of the door lining and into the studwork around the lining. For block or brick walls, some masonry nails may be required.

5 Continue by measuring off the vertical architrave requirements. This can be done very precisely by holding a length of the architrave, which is slightly longer than the door height, wrong side out and butted against the edge of the top length of fixed architrave. Then make a mark with a sharp pencil where the vertical length meets the horizontal one, and use this as an accurate guideline when you use the mitresaw to cut the length to the required size.

6 You can now nail the vertical lengths in position. Add one further nail into each architrave corner joint, inserting the nail through one section of the architrave and into the adjacent piece. This helps to hold the mitred joints tightly together and reduces the risk of them splitting open at a later date.

7 Finally use a hammer and nail punch to ensure that nail heads are knocked in below the surface level of the architrave.

tips of the trade

• Although a mitresaw has been used to cut the architrave in the example shown here, an alternative method is to measure the distance required and use a panel saw and mitre block to achieve a clean 45 degree cut.

• When preparing a finished door frame for decoration, use a flexible filler to seal the gap along the outside edges of the architrave and the mitred joins, to allow for any slight movement in the door frame once it is in use.

front door fittings ⚒

Aside from the basic handles, front doors often require further fittings, which are not necessary on internal doors. Although these fittings have a functional job to perform, they also add a decorative aspect to the front door and exterior of the house as a whole. Extra care should always be taken when working on them as mistakes can be very costly.

tools for the job

tape measure

pencil

combination square

cordless drill/driver

jigsaw

pliers

hammer

fitting a letterbox

The positioning of a letterbox is to a large extent determined by front door design. Fitting can take place when the door is hung in position, but it is often easier to carry it out with the door laid flat on trestle supports.

1 On the outer side of the door, mark out a rectangular guideline slightly larger than the plate of the letterbox on the middle of the central rail. Then mark crosses far enough in from each corner to accommodate the diameter of the drill bit. The drill hole should be large enough to accommodate a jigsaw blade.

2 Drill through the door at each cross with an auger or flat drill bit, ensuring that the hole does not extend outside the guideline. When drilling through, hold a block of wooden offcut tightly against the other side of the door where the drill point will emerge. This will prevent any wood being split or blown out on the other side.

3 Cut along the pencil guideline with a jigsaw, beginning each cut from one of the drilled holes. Remove the block of wood, then smooth any rough edges with fine grade sandpaper. Next, mark out the position of the retaining bolts.

4 Drill holes for the retaining bolts, holding a wooden block on the opposite side of the door to prevent splitting. Often letterbox design requires holes on the exterior of the door to be widened slightly at, and just below, surface level in order to accommodate the letterbox plate, so two sizes of drill bit may be required.

5 Attach the retaining bolts to the letterbox and thread them through the holes to the other side of the door.

6 Turn the door over and screw the retaining nuts onto the bolts. (Tighten with pliers if necessary.)

A doorknocker is fixed using a similar principle to a letterbox, again involving bolts that extend through the door and are secured by nuts on the inside face. Positioning is again affected by door design, but for panel doors, a central position where the top door rail crosses the vertical central stile is always a suitable place for a doorknocker.

1 Measure out the central position for the knocker and strike plate, making a clear pencil cross to act as a guideline for drilling.

2 Drill through the door, holding a wooden offcut on the other side to prevent damage to the wood. You may need to use a second, slightly larger drill bit to open up the entrance holes in order to accommodate the knocker and strike plate design.

3 Screw the supplied bolts into the retaining holes of both the knocker and strike plate, ensuring that the bolts are inserted straight, so that the risk of crossthreading is thereby reduced.

4 Insert both the knocker and strike plate through the appropriate holes, turn the door over and tighten the retaining bolts to secure the doorknocker in place. When positioning the knocker, a tap with the butt end of a hammer or a wooden mallet may be required, as the knocker is often designed with a small point behind its face which pierces into the door surface and adds to the security of the fixing. It is also best to cover the face of the knocker with a cloth when carrying out this process to prevent scratching or damaging the knocker surface finish.

The practical and aesthetically pleasing combination of external door furniture can add tremendous decorative appeal to the overall look of a front door.

installing cylinder locks ⚡⚡⚡

Cylinder rim locks are among the most common types of lock for front doors. From a security angle they are very effective, but are always best when combined with other door security features (see pages 70–71). Designs do vary but the basic principle of cylinder rim locks remains the same, in that a locking barrel extends through the door and combines with a latch to form a closing mechanism operated by key from the outside and with a lever from the inside.

tools for the job

pencil
combination square
cordless drill/driver
screwdrivers
hammer
mini hacksaw
chisel

1 On the inside of the door, draw a horizontal pencil guideline across the closing stile of the door. Use a combination square to continue this line around the edge and onto the front of the door. The exact height positioning for a cylinder rim lock is not standardized, but it should be on the upper half of the door – 1m 30cm (4ft 3in) from the floor is generally an acceptable height to fit it.

2 Use the combination square to measure the distance between the lock edge (closest to the latch) and the hole that will accommodate the flat connecting bar. Lock the combination square in position at this exact point. Then transfer this measurement to the door, opening it slightly and resting the edge of the combination square against the door edge, whilst marking off the position on the horizontal pencil guideline.

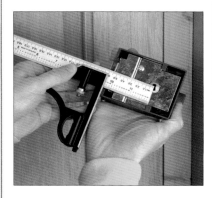

3 Use an auger or flat bit to drill through the door at the marked point. The size of bit required will normally be suggested on the lock packaging and relates directly to the size of the cylinder for the lock. It is best to drill from both sides to make the holes because otherwise the re-emerging drill bit can make splits in the wood surface. Alternatively, whilst drilling, hold an offcut tight against the other side of the door, corresponding to where the drill bit will appear.

4 On the exterior of the door, insert the cylinder through its brass ring and the drilled hole, so that the flat connecting bar extends through to the other side of the door.

5 Fix the mounting plate to the cylinder and the inside of the door ensuring that it is level, and that the edge of the plate is aligned precisely with the door edge. It may be necessary to make pilot holes for the screw fixings, especially if you are using a hardwood door, which is what is shown here. When drilling the pilot holes, be sure that you are extremely accurate and also make certain that the drill bit goes into the door surface absolutely level.

6 Depending on door depth, the flat connecting bar may be too long to allow for the easy positioning of the lock. It may therefore be necessary to trim the bar back so that the lock may be fitted. A mini hacksaw is the ideal tool for this purpose. Double-check your cutting measurements because you will not be able to rectify mistakes later.

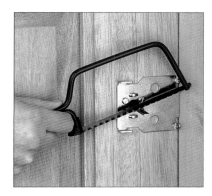

7 Push the lock case onto the mounting plate, shifting it along until it catches firmly in position. This precise fitting procedure may vary slightly between different designs, and although the fit itself is very tight, there is normally a simple procedure for sliding the casing in place. Once in position, insert the two retaining screws to secure the lock casing firmly on the door.

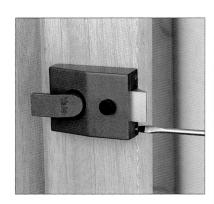

8 Next, close the door and draw a straight guideline above and below the lock casing on the door frame. A torpedo level can be used for this process, but space is very often confined, and therefore you may find

that it is actually easier to use the straight edge of the staple itself to aid you in this marking-up process.

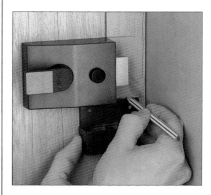

9 Open the door and hold the staple in place, following the guidelines you have just made. Continue the guideline round onto the internal facing of the door frame.

10 Measure the recessed part of the staple and transfer the measurement to the frame. This shows what wood must be removed to accommodate the staple. Use a chisel to cut the area, taking care not to damage the surrounding wood.

11 Finally, position the staple in the recess and screw it in place on the frame. Test the door to make sure the rim lock closes and opens correctly, making any minor adjustments as required.

RIM LOCK GUIDELINES

• **Standards** – Only ever fit a rim lock that is supplied in packaging and displays the relevant approval badges and assertions. Also check that the lock comes with a guarantee.

• **Dual use** – Although rim locks are a common front door feature, they are ideal for any other external door.

• **Decorative choice** – Security features such as this are never going to be attractive, but do consider that, like most fittings, locks can be bought in a number of different finishes.

• **Stile check** – Check the dimensions of the door stile to make sure the lock casing will fit onto it. Otherwise, a slimmer lock than that shown here will be required.

• **Dead lock** – The rim lock shown here has a dead lock option so that, once it has been locked with the key, it will not be possible to open the door. This is essential for doors with glass panes, so if a thief does break a pane and reach the lock, they will still be unable to open the door. For obvious safety reasons, key-operated dead locks must not be used when people are left inside the home.

fitting extra security

Security fittings for doors, and front doors especially, stretch further than just rim locks, and there are a number of other systems which may be used to add to the security offered by a rim locking mechanism. It is not necessary to use all the features shown here on a single door, but a combination of these items will make you feel safer in your own home.

tools for the job

pencil
tape measure
cordless drill/driver
chisel
bradawl
screwdrivers
torpedo level

mortice door bolts

Mortise door bolts are straightforward to fit and offer an excellent security mechanism for external doors. They are operated by a specially shaped key which extends the bolt between the door and frame when moved to the locking position. These door bolts may be fitted on a hanging door or on one of its hinges, as shown here.

1 Holding the barrel of the door bolt, draw a guideline around its faceplate on the door edge. Ensure that the rectangular guideline drawn is central to the edge of the door.

2 Using the correct size of auger or flat drill bit (size should be on the packaging), drill vertically down into the door edge. Make sure that the drill remains completely vertical, otherwise operation of the bolt will be hindered. Drill to a depth equal to that of the door bolt.

3 Chisel out inside the rectangular pencil guideline to a depth equal to that of the door bolt face plate. Make cuts with the chisel along the shorter dimensions of the rectangle (across the grain) before making cuts along the longer dimensions (with the grain). This will help prevent any splitting of the wood.

4 Hold the door bolt on the face of the door, aligning it with the drilled hole in the edge. Use a bradawl to mark the face of the door at the position on the bolt where the key will be inserted. Drill into the door at this point, allowing the drill to extend only as far as the door bolt hole in the edge of the door. Make sure you do not continue to drill through to the other side of the door.

5 Fit the door bolt in place in the edge of the door, securing it in place with the retaining screws. It may be necessary to drill pilot holes for the screws before inserting them.

6 Finally, fit the key plate on the face of the door so that its hole aligns directly with the one in the door. Another mortise door bolt may now be fitted at the bottom level of the door, before it is rehung on the door frame. Both bolts will need holes and cover plates positioned in the door frame. A similar technique to that for fitting a door latch strike plate is used here, where the position for the plate is marked off and the appropriate amount of chiselling out is carried out to accommodate the door bolt.

door bolts

Simple door bolts offer a further option to the mortise door bolt. These are surface mounted and are even simpler to fit. Again, it is wise to have door bolts positioned at both the top level and bottom level of the door.

1 Hold the bolt in position on the door, using a torpedo level to make sure that it is perfectly horizontal. Use a bradawl to mark the positions for the screws on the face of the door.

2 Pilot drill holes and then screw the bolt in place. The same marking procedure can be used to position the catch plate for the bolt on the door frame. Take great care when using screws with solid brass fittings because a simple slip with the screwdriver may scratch the brass

surface and therefore detract from the finished look of the job once it has been completed.

peep holes

Door security does not necessarily have to involve a lock or mechanical barrier of some nature, as the use of peep holes demonstrates. These security items are simply used to check the identity of a caller even before opening the door.

1 Peep holes are normally supplied with both sections screwed together. Undo the two components and select a drill bit slightly larger than the size of the thread in the peep hole.

2 Drill a hole in the door centrally at eye level on the middle door stile. On the outside of the door insert the correct piece of the peep hole.

3 Turn the door over and insert the other section of the peep hole, screwing it in position into the

other section. The flat edge of a screwdriver may be required for tightening purposes. Although this peep hole has been installed with the door off its hinges, these security devices can also be installed with the door still hung in place.

door chains

These useful fixtures allow the door to be opened slightly, so that visitor identity can be checked before the door is opened fully. Door limiters are another version of this system.

1 The chain is best positioned at an appropriate height around the middle section of the door. Just below the rim lock is ideal. Use a bradawl to mark the position and then screw the main chain plate onto the door.

2 Attach the chain and retaining plate to the door frame, positioning it so that the chain can be conveniently slipped in place on the main chain plate.

changing door appearance

From time to time, it can be desirable to change the appearance of doors in your home without going to the effort and expense of full replacement. Decorative changes are outlined further on pages 98–111, but it is possible to renovate doors, or change their appearance to something more appealing, in ways other than simply painting. These pages explain how to make and fit decorative panels to a flush door, adding simple, but attractive texture to the door surface.

renovating a flush door

Flush doors can be considered relatively featureless examples of door design. In some cases, this may be the minimalist look required. There is always the option, however, of adding panels to an existing flush door, which provides greater character at half the cost of full replacement with authentic panel doors. Expense can even be saved by adding panels to a relatively cheap new flush door.

panel considerations

Before starting you should first consider how many panels are going to be required on the door surface. Choices are normally either four panels of a similar size or six panels with the top two being around half the size of the lower four. Bear in mind that the greater the number of panels, the larger the amount of moulding and

the greater the number of cuts, that will be required. This is a particularly important consideration if you are panelling throughout your home and on both sides of doors, because the expense can escalate rapidly.

The choice of moulding also varies in style as well as price. The most ornate varieties can be expensive and often the cheaper, simpler designs are all that is required to achieve an effective panel door. As mouldings are normally painted, wood quality is not an essential consideration, so long as the mouldings are not split.

tools for the job

paint brush
combination square
pencil
tape measure
spirit level
mitresaw
scissors or craft knife

1 On a new door, it is always best to prime the surface before attaching the panels. The primer

improves adhesion between the mouldings and the door when the double-sided tape is applied and the mouldings are positioned.

2 In addition to the door itself, it is also worth priming the moulding lengths before they are cut to fit. This saves time later, and also improves adhesion for the same reasons as explained in step 1.

3 Once the primer has dried, accurately measure the door size and begin by marking off what will be the outer corner points of the panels. A combination square is an ideal aid for this process and helps to keep measurements precise.

tips of the trade

If the mouldings are to be picked out in a different colour from the rest of the door surface, it is best to apply undercoat and top coat to the mouldings before they are cut to size, and to paint the flush door surface with undercoat and top coat as well. This done, the mouldings can be attached so that the only paint requirement will be a 'touch up' of the coats already applied. Thus the very fiddly 'cutting in' requirement of the two differing colours on the door will be avoided, speeding up the time taken to complete the task by a considerable margin.

4 Use a spirit level to draw the pencil guidelines. Keeping these lines vertical or horizontal as required makes the panelling process much easier to achieve. Once all the panels are marked out on the door surface, measure each panel dimension separately and use a mitresaw to cut lengths of moulding to size. Accuracy at this stage will help to eliminate the need for any filling on mitre joins once the panels are in place.

5 Apply double-sided tape to the back of the moulding. Ensure that the tape runs all the way, centrally, along its length and that there are no wrinkles or unevenness in the tape surface. Remove the backing from the tape once positioned, so that it may then be stuck to the door surface. The double-sided tape can be cut using scissors or a craft knife.

6 Attach the mouldings, with the outside edge of the moulding running along the pencil guidelines. The adhesive properties of the tape should allow for some adjustment of position when first placed on the door surface, though the glue will soon set, creating a tight bond between moulding and door surface. Continue to apply lengths until all panels are complete.

PANELLING TIPS

• **Filling** – So long as measurements are accurate, there should only be limited filling requirements on the mouldings before decoration can take place. Use flexible filler or caulk to fill any slightly open mitre joints, and along any open joins between the moulding edges and the door face.

• **Nailing alternative** – Instead of using double-sided tape, it is possible to attach the mouldings using panel pins. However, the panel pin heads will require filling and sanding once they are hammered in place. Apply a small amount of wood glue to the back of the mouldings before they are positioned, to ensure that a good bond is achieved.

• **Ready-made panels** – Some manufacturers produce completed panels which can be attached directly to the door surface, eliminating the need for you to make mitred cuts. However, while these kits are very useful they can be expensive.

Combining colour can help to enhance the appearance of a panel door and draw further attention to its texture and design.

fitting door closers ⟋⟋⟋

Door closers are essential pieces of equipment used primarily in the domain of fire doors, whereby the automatic door closer mechanism acts to shut the door to maintain the desired fire barrier at all times. Door closers may also be used on standard doors where automatic closing is needed. These closers can either be visible or concealed from view.

tools for the job

bradawl

cordless drill/driver

chisels

tape measure

combination square

pliers

fitting a hydraulic door closer

These are the most common of the visible variety and are generally positioned at the top of the door and frame. The hydraulic mechanism is enclosed in a casing, which is attached to the top of the door and joined to the frame by a pivoting bar. As well as pulling the door shut, the mechanism also controls the speed at which the door closes. Designs can vary slightly, but most are based on principles similar to those demonstrated here.

1 Most such door closers will come supplied with a paper template to help position the casing. Attach the template to the door, securing it in place with some masking tape. Ensure the template is the right way round for the way the door is opening, and that its edges are perfectly aligned with those of the door. Use a bradawl to mark the fixing positions for the casing, making slight indents through the template and into the door surface. At the same time,

mark the positions for the retaining bracket for the door closer arm on the architrave.

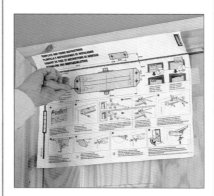

2 Pilot drill holes for the casing and screw it in position on the door surface. Take extra care to ensure that the door closer casing is the right way up and accurately positioned using the template hole guidelines.

3 Depending on the architrave design, it may be necessary to cut out a small section of wood from the architrave, so that the door closer arm bracket can be fixed flush in position. Draw an outline for the bracket and drill pilot holes, so that

once wood has been chiselled out it will still be possible to see the holes for screw insertion.

4 Attach the first section of the closer arm to the bracket and screw it in place on the architrave. Again, check that the bracket and arm are positioned the right way up, as subtle differences may hamper you from determining this.

5 Attach the other section of arm to the door closer casing and join it to the first arm with the nut and bolt supplied. Small adjustments may be necessary for exact positioning.

6 Open the door and allow it to close. It may be necessary to adjust the tension to suit your requirements. Most such door closers can be adjusted with a slot-head screwdriver, inserted at a special point on the side of the door closer.

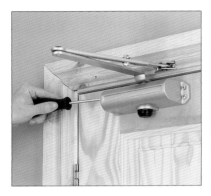

concealed door closers

With the function and workings hidden whilst the door is closed, this variety of door closer can be considered far more aesthetically pleasing than the type shown opposite. However, depending on door weight and its overall dimensions, more than one concealed door closer may be needed to fulfil the automatic closing function.

1 Open up the door and mark a cross in the middle of the door edge, central to the door's middle rail.

2 Drill at right angles and perfectly horizontally into the door at the point of the cross just marked. Use a drill bit equal to the size of the barrel

of the door closer. Drill bit size will normally be printed on the packaging. An auger or flat bit may be used for this purpose. Only drill in as far as the length of the door closer itself.

3 Insert the door closer in the hole and use a pencil to mark around the edge of the face plate. Ensure that the face plate is precisely vertical for the pencil guideline.

4 Chisel out a recess to accommodate the depth of the face plate. Working close to the door edge like this means that extra care is required not to split the wood.

5 Use the face plate of the door closer to draw another guideline on the door lining surface. Chisel out this area to the depth required for the door closer anchor plate.

6 Use pliers to pull the anchor plate away from the face plate, and insert the retaining bar across the chain to prevent it closing. Now insert the door closer in the door.

7 Finally, screw the anchor plate in place. Carefully remove the retaining bar from the chain and allow the door to close automatically. Tension may be adjusted if necessary.

insulating doors

Most doors suffer from draught problems, especially given that the opening and closing mechanism will not function efficiently without gaps around the door edges. Pvc and double glazed doors offer the best insulation, but with wooden doors it is often necessary to take further measures to improve insulation and reduce unwanted draughts. Such insulating techniques may be applied to both exterior and interior doors, although the materials used tend to differ.

exterior strips

An effective option used on many exterior doors is to attach draught excluder strips to the door frame. When the door is closed, a slight overlap of the strip from the door onto the frame effectively closes the gap that a draught may otherwise penetrate through. Designs vary, but most draught excluder strips are fitted using the technique shown below.

tools for the job

tape measure

craft knife

hammer

nail punch

1 Cut the strips to size so that you have one for each upright of the door frame and one length for the top of the frame. Mitred corners provide a good join between the strips. Position them ensuring that the more flexible edge of each section touches and follows the profile of the door surface.

2 Pin the strips in place, ensuring contact between them and the door surface when the door is in a closed position. Since the nails or pins used are so small, it is often easier to knock them into their final position using a punch. This also reduces the risk of damaging the strip with the hammer.

insulating tape

An alternative to the exterior strips is to use insulating tapes which are positioned on the internal part of the frame or on the doorstop. The advantage of these is that they are not visible when the door is in a

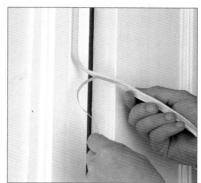

closed position and are also particularly easy to apply. Always read the manufacturer's guidelines to determine their recommended positioning, as tape design does vary and they may be used in slightly different positions on the frame or door surface.

Most insulating or excluder tapes are self-adhesive and are secured in place by peeling away the backing and pressing the strip into position. The adhesive used on these tapes is quick acting, so take care to position the tape correctly on first application as later adjustment is not always possible.

frame/wall junctions

Another area for draught penetration can be between the door frame and surrounding masonry. It is particularly important to close up such gaps, as these are also areas where damp or moisture can penetrate, leading to further problems.

tools for the job

sealant gun

masking tape

1 In order to make a neat finish, it is best to use masking tape. Apply separate strips of tape along the length of the junction on both the wall and frame. Even though the wall or masonry surface may be slightly rough or undulating, try to smooth

the tape into all depressions and recesses, whilst still maintaining a precise vertical edge to it.

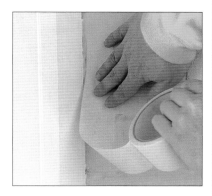

2 Load the sealant gun with a tube of silicone sealant. Cut the nozzle so that its diameter is slightly wider than the gap between the two lengths of masking tape. Depress the trigger and expel an even bead of sealant along the junction.

3 Smooth the sealant with a wetted finger, and proceed to remove the masking tape. The tape must be removed immediately after application, before the sealant dries.

A common measure to reduce draughts and improve insulation is to use draught excluder strips on internal doors.

tools for the job

tape measure
mini hacksaw
bradawl
screwdriver

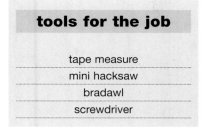

1 Strips are supplied in lengths greater than standard door size so it is therefore necessary to cut them down to size before screwing in place. Measure the width of the base of the door and cut down the metal section of the excluder strip using a mini hacksaw.

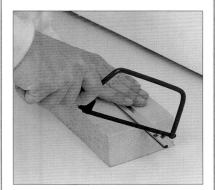

2 Insert the supplied brushes into the strip and position at the base of the door. Make pilot holes for the fixings using a bradawl. Make sure the strip is positioned so that

when the door is in a closed position the brushes rest on the floor, thereby cutting out any draught penetration under the door.

3 Screw the strip in place, again to ensure that the brushes make good contact with the floor surface. If need be, make adjustments before tightening the screws.

SOUND INSULATION

As well as insulating for draught reduction, it is possible to insulate with sound reduction in mind. All the measures shown here will certainly help with sound insulation but there are further methods that can be employed.

• **Door quality** – If sound insulation is a priority then door quality must be a consideration. As a general rule, doors of higher quality will tend to be more solid and therefore their sound insulating properties are enhanced. So door replacement is always an option.

• **Increasing depth** – As a less drastic measure, door depth can sometimes be increased to improve sound insulation. Simply fitting ply sheets to the surface of the door will help reduce sound transference between rooms.

• **Sound insulation strips** – Proprietary sound insulation strips can be purchased and fixed in a similar way to that shown for the draught excluder strips.

fitting windows

Fitting windows involves both internal and external considerations, so there are many areas to be considered when working on their installation. In many cases the projects may involve replacing more than one window and therefore planning your work and adhering to a timetable becomes a crucial factor. Remember that aesthetic considerations are just as important on the outside as they are on the inside, and there are the added factors of ensuring that the best security is employed, and that the window is able to deal with all manner of attack from the elements, through weatherproofing measures such as insulation and draft proofing. This chapter looks at all these concerns and explains the best techniques for installation of both full window units, and the various accessories which are used to complete the window function.

This window has been fitted with wooden beads to leave a neat finish between the framework and panes.

choosing options

When replacing old windows with new, options can be slightly limited due to size specification. There is still a range of choices here, mainly relating to the type of opening system a window employs, and its finish on both interior and exterior surfaces. The examples shown here are provided to give a basic overview of window options, and it should be remembered that there are wide variations in style between manufacturers. You should also bear in mind issues of planning permission.

wooden windows

Wooden window quality is determined mainly by whether the wood used in its construction is softwood or hardwood. Both options have their advantages and disadvantages. Softwood windows are much cheaper and therefore more economical to use, especially if you are replacing a large number of windows. However, they are not as hardwearing or durable as hardwood windows which, though much more expensive, will definitely outlast the lifespan of softwood equivalents. Price is also determined by the complexity of design, so that small paned windows are more expensive than large paned windows of a similar overall unit size, because there is clearly more work and wood involved in their construction.

casement (large pane)

Large pane casements are competitively priced and a very popular choice of wooden window. Large panes allow maximum light into the house.

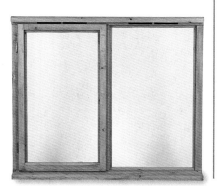

casement (small pane)

These casements offer greater character than large pane equivalents. Although the installation procedure for the unit as a whole is similar to a large pane casement, fitting the glass will take considerably longer.

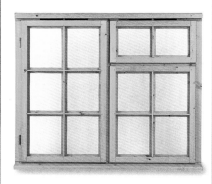

sash (large pane)

Large pane sashes demonstrate similar properties to large pane casements, but with a different opening mechanism. Many new sash windows will be operated by a spiral balance mechanism rather than the more traditional system of cords and pulleys.

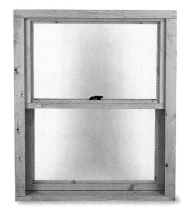

sash (small pane)

Small pane sashes are more complex in design, and variation on the 'light' size can offer further interest in terms of overall style.

picture window

Large fixed casement windows, or openers as shown here, are simple in design and allow the maximum amount of light into a room. They may also be top or bottom hinged. Some are even hinged centrally along the vertical rails so that the opening mechanism is a pivot action. This system may also be referred to as a tilting action.

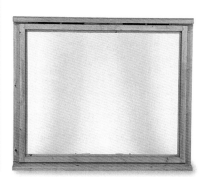

arch

Unusual designs such as arched windows tend to be supplied in some standard sizes by manufacturers, but for unusual styles it may be necessary to get windows handmade to size, which can clearly be an expensive option. However, shapes or designs such as this provide an attractive architectural feature.

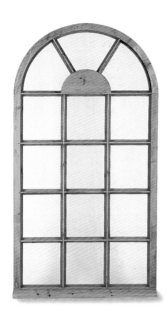

pvc windows

Pvc windows have become hugely popular in today's market, mainly due to their weatherproof and insulatory properties. Designs vary dramatically between manufacturers, with many of the styles shown in the wooden window section opposite also available in pvc. Quality is often related to the security aspects of the window, as window furniture and locking mechanisms are built into the design before installation, unlike most wooden windows where these aspects are often fixed in place after the main window unit has been installed. Price also varies according to the number of opening units a window has, the complication in design and the glass used. Options are therefore many and varied.

pvc

This pvc window has a simple top-opening casement design with the bottom casement fixed. Opening designs and mechanisms vary hugely and are chosen according to personal preference. Because pvc is such a popular choice in today's market, there are a huge number of suppliers and as such the price and quality of product can vary considerably. It is well worth shopping around to get the best deal and find the right compromise between price and quality.

metal windows

Metal windows in the traditional sense are far less common than in years gone by, and it is rare for them to be used in a new installation. Aluminium. double glazed units are still used in some properties but the move has definitely been more towards pvc equivalents, which are cheaper to make and install.

material combinations

Some manufacturers produce windows that combine materials to create specific designs and styles. For example, aluminium casement windows are sometimes combined with wooden frames, or double glazed units with wooden window frames.

roof windows

These offer a further example of material combination, with the wooden opening section of a roof window often combined with a metal-based frame during installation. These types of windows are used in sloping roofs and are therefore a common choice for loft conversions. Comprehensive fitting instructions are generally supplied by the manufacturer with the window.

hinging mechanisms

As with all building design, innovation and changes are constantly being introduced in order to try to improve or update existing ideas or mechanisms. Hinges for windows are a good example in this regard. In many newer properties, traditional hinge mechanisms for casement windows are no longer used because of a move towards projecting or friction hinges. These tend to be the standard type of hinge used in pvc windows, but they are certainly now incorporated in many modern wooden windows. In most cases they eliminate the need for windows to have stays and pins to hold them in an open position and therefore only casement fasteners are required.

window furniture & security fittings

Most new wooden windows are supplied with window furniture, but it is often relatively cheap and simple in design, and there is always the option to change it for something more decorative. Security fittings will also need to be added to wooden windows to ensure they are easy to lock and safe from intruders. Pvc and metal windows tend to be supplied with window furniture as part of the window design and therefore options should be chosen at the same time as the windows.

security fittings

Security fittings are required for both casement and sash windows, and in a growing market there are many options to suit particular needs and window designs. Some are combined with window opening and closing mechanisms, such as locking casement fasteners or locking sash window fasteners. Other fittings operate independently of the main fittings and represent a supplementary mechanism.

sliding sash window lock

sliding sash window bolt with plate casement

casement locking stay pin

sliding sash window bolt

casement window lock (automatic locking)

locking casement fastener (mortise)

locking casement fastener (wedge)

INSURANCE

It is worth bearing in mind that many insurance companies will specify the lock type to be used on windows and doors. You should therefore check your policy to see if there is any stipulation before going ahead and fitting security systems.

locking sash window fastener

casement window lock

safety advice

Make sure that all members of the household know where the window keys are kept. Ideally, there should be one in each room for in the event of an emergency, quick access may be vital.

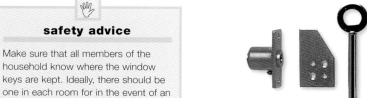
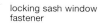

sash window stop

mortise window bolt

Casement fittings are based on fasteners and stays, primarily because these are the tried and tested mechanisms for both closing and opening windows and allowing them to be opened and locked at a certain distance. Trickle vents are also now installed in new windows to increase room ventilation. When choosing window furniture, ensure that the dimension of window rails is suitable for the furniture you choose as the size of the fixing plate for fasteners and stays does vary.

scroll fastener

Victorian fastener

black wrought iron fastener

telescopic sliding friction stay

window furniture & security fittings

83

trickle vent

screw-up stay for casements

black wrought iron stay and pins

brass casement stay and pins

Sash fittings have to operate in a completely different fashion to casement equivalents as the opening and closing mechanism for the window is very different. Since the distance a sash window can be opened is secured in position by the sash cord balance mechanism itself, the main function of sash window furniture is to fasten the window when shut, or to provide an area to grip onto for opening or closing. There is a wide selection of options available.

sash lift

sash eye

sash pulley with nylon wheel

sash lifting handle

ring sash lift

FANLIGHTS

Fanlights also require a catch mechanism similar to sashes and this has no involvement in the distance a window stays open. These catches normally fall into two categories:

fanlight – catch plate   fanlight – catch box

sash stop

sash fastener – unsprung

sash fastener – fitch

sash fastener – quadrant arm

fitting a window – 1 ✐✐

Fitting a window, or replacing an old one with a new, is a two-part process of initial removal followed by installation – removal often being the more arduous part of the project. Before removal always check that the new window is the right size: discovering that it does not fit after the old one has been taken out may mean you have to board up the opening temporarily.

window removal

Before starting work it is best to check that the weather forecast is favourable, since opening your home to the elements is an inescapable consequence of window replacement. In this example an old metal window is being taken out. Wooden windows tend to be much simpler to remove as they can be sawn or cut out much more easily than metal, which requires the use of more heavy duty cutting equipment. However, in both cases the aim must be to remove the entire existing window and frame, back to the masonry surround.

tools for the job

protective equipment
grinder
hammer
old chisel or screwdriver
nail punch
hacksaw
wrecking bar
dusting brush

1 Remove any opening casements from the window. On wooden windows, this can be achieved by unscrewing the hinges to release the casements. On metal windows, the hinges are normally externally positioned and cannot be undone in the same manner as for wooden ones – they must be physically cut away from the main frame. The best tool for this is a grinder whose rotating blade can be used to cut though the metal hinge. Grinders can be hired quite cheaply from your local hire shop. Remember to follow all the manufacturer's instructions and guidelines for use.

2 Once all opening casements have been removed, apply masking tape over the glass in the remaining fixed casements. Proceed to remove the glass panes by initially knocking away any loose putty around the edges of the panes, using a hammer and old chisel or screwdriver. At the same time, you should be

looking for the screw or bolt heads on the horizontal rails that join the various sections of the metal window together. Look for fixings on the outer side of the window frame as well – these are for attachment to the wall surface. Generally, most of the glass has to be removed to expose these fixing points.

3 When fixings are found, use a hammer and nail punch to knock the screw or bolt out of the frame. A few firm knocks with the hammer should loosen it.

4 Once the head of the screw or bolt is exposed, it can be easier to use the claw of the hammer to lever it out of the frame. Alternatively, the claw end of a wrecking bar may be used to do this.

5 Almost invariably, the fixings around the edge of the window, which are attached to the wall, are not so easy to shift. This is mainly because they are longer and more heavy duty in order to secure the

window in place. You may therefore need to use a grinder to cut off the fixing heads. Once the head is off, a few knocks with a hammer and punch on the remaining fitting should knock it clear from the frame, releasing the window edge from its fixed position.

6 The fixed sections of the window may be further broken down by once more using the grinder to cut through the uprights of the vertical rails.

7 If vibration of the rail or window unit as a whole becomes too intense to make use of the grinder

effective, it may be easier to finish these cuts using a normal hacksaw.

8 The removal of the fixings in the horizontal part of the window frame, combined with the cuts in the vertical framework, now makes it possible to pull the relevant sections of the window frame apart. A wrecking bar is the ideal tool to help lever the sections apart.

9 Once the central areas have been broken down, it now becomes easier to lever the frame away from the masonry surround of the window. Again, a wrecking bar is ideal for this job. You may find the odd frame fixing which you missed during the initial removal process. Simply use the grinder to remove fixing heads as necessary and pull the frame from the wall surface.

10 Check around the edge of the window opening to ensure that no remnants of frame fixings are still attached. Remove them with a claw hammer should any be

found, at the same time taking care not to cause damage to the masonry surface. Any fixings that are likely to remove large portions of masonry when levered out should be removed using the grinder instead.

11 Once the entire window framework has been removed and the aperture is totally clear, brush and then dust around the entire frame to remove any debris and loose material. A standard decorator's dusting brush may be used to provide a totally clear surface for the installation of the new window.

safety advice

Taking out windows requires some caution as glass will almost certainly be broken. It is therefore essential to wear gloves and goggles for protection against glass and other flying debris. Also, hang a dust sheet close to the window inside the house to keep mess to a minimum, and always tidy away any broken glass as soon as possible, both inside and outdoors.

fitting a window – 2 ⁊⁊⁊⁊

The technique for fitting wooden or pvc windows is very similar – the most important part of installation being to ensure that the new window is positioned in exactly the same place as the old one. In houses that have cavity walls, it may also be necessary to renew the damp proof course around the edge of the opening before inserting the new window.

fitting a new pvc window

Windows may arrive glazed or partially glazed. Check the instructions, as some will advise removing glass before installation and others may suggest only removing glass from fixed casements. You may also need to attach the windowsill to the frame before installation.

tools for the job

spirit level
cordless drill/driver
sealant gun
hammer
mini hacksaw

1 Windows will almost certainly be supplied covered with protective tape to prevent any scratches or damage in transit and prior to installation. This can now be removed before the window is fitted – the protective layers should simply peel away from the main pvc frame.

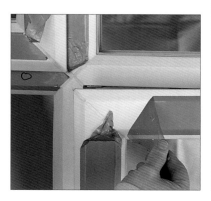

2 Position the window in the aperture and use a spirit level to ensure it is vertical and horizontal. For large windows two people may be required for this process, with one checking the spirit level while the other makes minor adjustments. Once you are satisfied the positioning is correct, use small wooden wedges to hold the window in place.

3 Secure the window in position with frame fixings that will penetrate at least 4cm (1½in) into the surrounding brick, blockwork or stone. Drill a pilot hole for the fixings directly through the window frame, using the correct size of drill bit.

4 Insert the frame fixing and, using a sealant gun, place a dab of silicone on the fixing hole – this will provide a seal once the fixing has been secured in place. Frame fixings will normally require one or two knocks with a hammer to position them in the hole. Stop using the hammer once the wall plug becomes flush with the surrounding frame.

5 Drive the screw into place, ensuring that the thread bites firmly into the wall plug and therefore the wall surface. Be careful not to overtighten the screw because this can cause the frame to bow and distort its shape. As you apply more frame fixings, keep checking with the spirit level that the window has not moved out of place, because it must be maintained in a vertical position.

6 Once all frame fixings have been inserted, attention can be directed towards glazing. This will generally require the use of packers in the rebates of each casement. These will be supplied with the window and should be positioned as per the manufacturer's guidelines, before the glazed units are inserted.

7 With packers in place, the glazed units can be slotted into place. A little pressure is often required to position the units. Also, if the unit has integral glazing bars, as the example here shows, ensure that they are straight. Snap the internal glazing beads into position once you are happy with the positioning of the glazed unit.

8 Once the whole window is glazed, it is necessary to deal with the junction between the window

frame and masonry. To hide any rough masonry edges, apply a bead of silicone around the sides of the frame, and press a pvc cover strip along the bead to secure it firmly in place. Cut the pvc cover strips to size using a mini hacksaw. Make good the recesses inside the house, with a bead of silicone around the frame.

9 Some windows may have drainage holes to let out any moisture from around the frame. Caps can be snapped in position on these holes to provide a more attractive finish to the window frame.

10 Finally, seal around the outer edge of the window frame and cover strips with a further bead of silicone sealant. The surface of the masonry is generally undulating, so it can be difficult to maintain an even and continuous line of sealant. The process can be aided by ensuring that the nozzle of the sealant tube is cut to the correct size, and if possible you can use masking tape to prevent excess sealant from spreading across the frame or masonry surface. Take plenty of time for this task as it certainly affects the finished look of the window.

Pvc windows are a practical alternative to traditional wooden varieties, they are maintenance free and they have become a common option for many homeowners.

measuring & cutting glass

In most cases, it is advisable and often more convenient to have glass cut by a supplier, especially if a considerable number of panes are required. Some varieties of glass, such as toughened or laminated, should always be cut by a professional. However, situations may arise where it is necessary to make glass cuts of your own, so it is important to understand the correct principles and techniques for carrying out this procedure.

measuring glass

It is vital that any measurements you take are extremely accurate, since glass has no flexibility and cannot easily be trimmed to size. Nor is it possible to join glass if a mistake in measurement has been made. A few simple guidelines must therefore be followed when obtaining measurements for cutting needs.

Bear in mind that glass is always bedded into a window or door frame, whether this be into putty or silicone (pvc windows are clearly excluded from this category). Any measurement must therefore leave a 1–2mm ($\frac{1}{16}$in) tolerance around the edge of the glass for this purpose. In apertures that have never had glass fitted, it is a simple case of measuring dimensions and subtracting the tolerance allowance.

For old windows where a cracked pane may need replacing, measurement is made more difficult as putty may obscure the exact edge of the aperture rebate, and therefore some estimation is required in making an accurate measurement. It is also worth remembering that, in older windows especially, the frame or apertures may not be totally 'square', so be sure to measure all the separate dimensions in order to reach the correct size requirements.

Since accuracy is so important, take extra care when measuring glass requirements and double-check everything before any cut is made. A little extra vigilance at this stage may save a great deal of time later on in the project as a whole.

tools for the job

cutting board

felt tip or Chinagraph pen

combination square

standard glass cutter

circular glass cutter

tape measure

scissors

cutting a simple pane

Cutting down a large pane of standard clear glass to a smaller size is a very straightforward process, provided you use a good quality glass cutter. Make sure that you have a firm, totally flat surface to work on – a piece of mdf board is ideal.

1 Use a felt tip or Chinagraph marker to mark the dimensions of the cut on the glass. A simple mark on the edge of the glass is all that is required, and always double-check the measurement as mistakes cannot be rectified. A combination square is an accurate measuring tool.

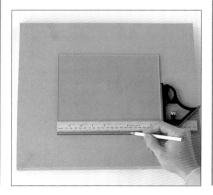

2 Holding a straight edge across the pane – again a combination square is an ideal tool here – score the surface of the glass with a glass cutter. Only score the surface once, making a precise line from one edge of the pane to the other.

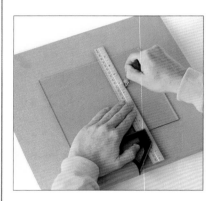

3 Wear goggles during the cutting process as a precaution against flying splinters of glass. Pick up the pane and position it on top of the combination square, so that the scored line runs precisely along the edge of the ruler of the square. Apply downward pressure to either side of the scored line, which will cause it to crack precisely along the line. The glass is now ready for fitting.

safety advice

Handling glass can cause severe personal injury and requires extreme caution. When working with glass, be sure to observe safety precautions and wear protective equipment when necessary.

cutting circles

A circular cut can often be required in such instances as vent installation in a window pane. Although this may sound difficult, cutting a circle uses the same principles as for cutting a straight line, except that the type of glass cutter used is slightly different. To achieve a circle, the head of the cutter needs to be fixed at right angles to the shaft, and there must also be a rubber sucker on the other end of the glass cutter to secure and pivot the cutter when in use.

1 Measure the radius requirement of the circular hole and transfer it to the glass cutter. It will be possible to adjust the position of the rubber sucker pad accordingly before securing it in place at the position required on the glass.

2 Secure the pad in the centre of the pane and carefully rotate the cutter around this central position to provide a scored outline. Again, this should only be done once, applying even and constant pressure to the

glass cutter head. You may also need to apply downward pressure to secure the rubber sucker in position.

3 Fix the glass cutter head back into a position perpendicular to the shaft, and make further scores in the glass surface inside the bounds of the scored circular guideline.

4 The scored glass circle will rarely come free in a single piece, so weaken the glass further, enabling it to be removed in smaller pieces. To do so, use the butt end of the glass cutter and tap in the central area until sections of glass begin to break free.

dealing with awkward shapes

The design of a window or door will sometimes demand glass panes of an irregular shape. This can make measurements for glass installation slightly more difficult. For such awkward shapes, the best technique is to make paper templates which may then be used as a guide for cutting purposes.

1 Tape a piece of paper or card over the aperture and draw a guideline around the edge of the aperture to provide an image of the required shape.

2 Cut out the shape accurately, making allowances for bedding in if required. Position the template in the frame aperture to check that it fits. When correct, take the template to a glass supplier who will have the specialist equipment to make such a complex cut. Do not try to cut a shape like this yourself.

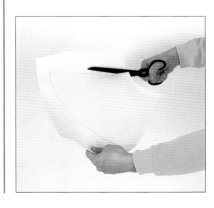

fitting glass

Fitting standard glass panes is a straightforward procedure which usually falls into one of two categories – installing either using putty or, alternatively, wooden beads. The former method is demonstrated in more detail on page 126, where a broken pane of glass is being replaced. The latter method is shown below and demonstrates the best technique for securing wooden beads.

fitting glass with beads

For new windows, manufacturers will often supply beads with the window, but in some cases it may be necessary to cut your own. The essential point to remember is that the beads must have a chamfered edge, so that when they are positioned water is taken away from the glass surface and prevented from collecting on the window rebates. Aside from this design necessity, the bead can be hardwood or softwood, which should generally be determined by the make-up of the window itself. Beads may also be used to secure double glazed units into wooden frames or apertures.

tools for the job

tape measure

sealant gun

cloth

mitresaw

hammer

card

nail punch

1 Even on a new window, check the dimensions of apertures to ensure that they are 'square'. On a window with multiple panes, it is often the case that not all will be of the same size. Often, those on the smaller opening casement are of a different size to the rest of the window, so be sure to check this situation before ordering or cutting glass. Once the

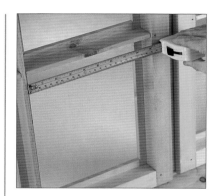

glass has been cut or supplied, check that the panes fit before proceeding any further.

2 With a sealant gun, run a bead of silicone around the complete rebate of the aperture. Make sure that the bead is continuous and there are no gaps. Silicone is supplied in a large range of colours – the clear variety is the most suitable for glazing purposes.

3 Take a pane of glass and position it in the aperture, by firstly bedding the bottom edge of the pane in the silicone sealant along the bottom rebate. From this starting

point, move your thumbs up the face of the pane, but close to its edges, gradually pressing it into place.

4 Carefully press the pane of glass in place ensuring that it fits correctly. Use a dry cloth to remove any excess silicone sealant.

tips of the trade

Silicone sealant is a notoriously sticky substance that can create a mess when an excessive amount is used. For large areas of overspill, use white spirit on a cloth to clean it away before it can dry.

5 Use a mitresaw with a fine blade to trim any beading as necessary. Apply another bead of silicone around the glass aperture rebate, and position the first wooden bead along the bottom edge. Push the bead into position, so that its face is flush against the glass surface and its base is sitting flush on the bottom wooden rebate.

6 Fit the top wooden bead followed by the side ones. The side beads may be a slightly tight fit, and you might need to tap them in place using the butt end of a hammer. However, take care not to force the beads as this could crack the glass (if they are simply too tight, saw off a sliver and refit them). Once the beads are fitted, again use a cloth to remove any excess sealant from the glass.

7 The beads should be secured in place using some glazing pins. Two on each bead is all that is required. Protect the glass surface from the edge of the hammer with a piece of card.

8 Finally, ensure that the glazing pins are flush with the wooden bead surface by using a nail punch for the final taps with the hammer.

pre-painting

In the example shown here, a natural wood finish means that there is no need to think about paint when installing the glass. Where a window requires painting, it is worth considering painting the beads before installation to reduce the time otherwise taken to cut-in paint next to the glass. It may also be advisable to paint the rebates before glass insertion. Depending on the thickness of glass used, it may be possible to see the bare wood at the bottom of the rebates, through the edge of the glass once it has been installed. Painting the rebates with the same colour as the window can help to avoid such an unsightly edge to the finished product. Also, it is worth bearing in mind that paint will not adhere to silicone so it may be worth pre-painting the beads before application. This means that any overspill of silicone will not affect the finished look of the final painted surface.

Wooden beads create a neat finish to wooden windows, making a clear and defined line between glass and frame.

installing window furniture

Clearly, for windows to function correctly they require some sort of window furniture to operate the various opening and closing mechanisms. Some new windows will come with window furniture fitted, and there is the option to use these or to change them to suit your personal tastes. A large selection of different types are shown on pages 82–3, but always undertake a few checks before making your final selection, as not all window furniture is suitable for every type of window.

fitting windows

fitting a casement fastener

Decide whether the fastener closes by means of a hook or mortise action. The former only requires surface mounting, whereas the latter needs to be cut into the window frame central upright. This is shown below.

tools for the job

bradawl
screwdriver
craft knife
chisel

1 Old furniture or, as in this case, the window furniture supplied with the new window, may simply be unscrewed and set aside before fitting new furniture. Hold the arm of the new fastener in the centre of the vertical casement rail. Use a pencil to mark through the screw holes onto the wood below. The height up the window will depend on window design. About halfway but below two-thirds is generally suitable.

2 Use a bradawl to make pilot holes at the pencil marks, then screw the fastener arm into position. Use a hand held screwdriver since a cordless driver has less control, and you risk allowing the driver head to slip off the head of the screw and scratch the brass fastener surface.

3 Bring the window to a closed position and hold the mortise plate of the fastener in place on the vertical casement frame. Position it so you can tell that the fastener arm will be able to close into the mortise, once the frame has been chiselled out. Draw around the plate with a sharp pencil, ensuring that the plate is in a precisely vertical position.

4 Cut around the pencil guideline with a craft knife, taking care not to allow the blade to slip. Cut to a depth equal to that of the fastener mortise plate. Use a chisel carefully to remove wood down to the depth of the mortise plate. This should be easily achieved by hand and not require the services of a hammer. Then hold the plate in place and draw a guideline inside the central area of the plate. Remove it once more and chisel the area out down to a depth that will allow the insertion of the fastener arm end.

5 Finally, place the mortise plate back in position, use a bradawl to make pilot holes once again, and screw it in securely.

hook fasteners

The main alternative to using mortise fasteners is to use hook fasteners. A similar technique is used to fit hook fasteners, except that the hook point of the fastener is surface mounted and does not need to be cut into the casement surface, unless the fastener design demands this to be the case. It is still important to position the hook point vertically on the central part of the casement frame and check that the fastener will close securely before screwing the hook point in place.

fitting stays and pins

As well as fasteners, most casements require stays to complete the opening and closing mechanism. Again, old or unwanted new window furniture should be removed, so that your chosen stays and pins may be fitted.

tools for the job

pencil
bradawl
screwdriver
cordless drill/driver

1 Close the window, securing it in place with the fitted fastener. Hold the stay in place along the bottom rail of the casement, marking the rail with a pencil through the screw holes in the stay securing plate.

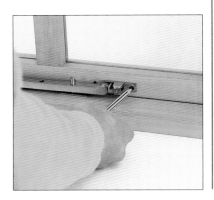

2 Use a bradawl to make pilot holes and then screw the stay in place, again by hand rather than cordless driver to avoid the risk of scratching the stay surface.

Mark the positions of the stay pins with a pencil. It may be necessary to hold the stay in a closed position to find the exact location required for fixing the pins in the correct place.

3 Make pilot holes at the pencil marks using a bradawl or fine drill bit as shown here. Screw the pins in position by hand and check the completed opening and closing mechanism of the window in its entirety. It is still possible at this late stage to adjust the pin position slightly to ensure that the stay closes onto the pins securely.

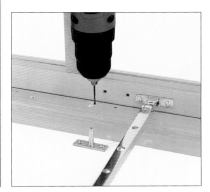

Although window furniture has a primarily functional role, it can also add a decorative edge to the finished look of a window.

adding security fittings

Although security fittings are usually seen as additional to standard opening and closing mechanisms, window furniture for security purposes ought to be regarded as equally important and just as 'standard', whilst issues of security should be considered for all varieties of window, not simply wooden casement windows. Again, there is a wide selection of fittings and you should choose according to the design of your windows and the finish of the other window furniture.

fitting casement locks

Some casement fasteners are supplied with an integral locking system (see page 83), but whether or not your windows have these fitted, casement locks further enhance the overall security set-up. Normally, two casement locks should be fitted to each casement with one at the bottom and one at the top of the vertical rail.

tools for the job

| bradawl |
| cordless drill/driver |
| screwdriver |

1 Hold the two sections of the lock mechanism in place on the window casement and frame. Use a bradawl to mark the fixing points for the lock on the casement.

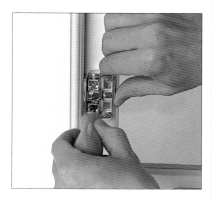

2 Use a cordless drill to drill pilot holes accurately in the casement. Ensure that the drill bit

used is smaller than the diameter of the screw shafts used for fitting the casement lock.

3 Screw the first part of the lock in position on the opening casement. Use a hand held screwdriver to provide better control than the cordless driver equivalent and reduce the risk of scratching the lock fitting.

4 Hold the second part of the casement lock in position on the vertical rail of the frame. Check its correct position by opening and closing the lock and, using a bradawl to mark its position, pilot hole these marks and screw the plate in place.

5 Finally, shut the window and use the supplied lock key to check that it closes correctly. Employ the same procedure to fit a further casement lock at the top level of the window.

fitting stay locks

There are many differing designs of stay lock available today, but one of the more common and most simple to fit is that which involves locking pins. In this situation, the original pins are being replaced by locking varieties, thus making the window more secure once it has been shut and locked.

tools for the job

bradawl

screwdriver

1 Release the stay from its closed position and unscrew the pins.

2 Hold the new locking pins in place and use a bradawl to mark new holes if necessary.

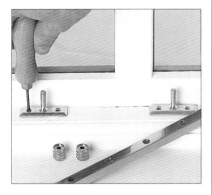

3 Screw the locking pins in place, ensuring that they are secured firmly in position on the frame.

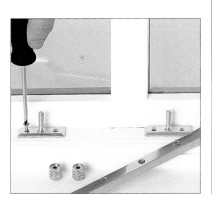

4 Close the stay and screw the locking barrels onto the threaded pins, securing them in place with the key supplied. These barrels will now rotate in position, unless a key is used to release them.

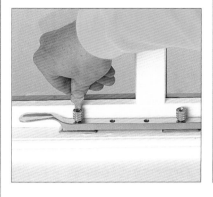

pvc windows

Pvc windows are usually supplied with both the standard furniture and security mechanisms built into the window design itself. Most pvc windows have locking fasteners, which in many designs have a number of locking points around the edge of any opening casements. These points are released or locked by the handle opening mechanism. So although security is in general already taken care of with pvc windows, there are few, if any, alternatives for changing window furniture after initial installation.

sash windows & security

Most sash window fittings have security built into their design, as demonstrated by the variety of fittings and options shown on page 83. However, the illustration below helps to demonstrate how sash window fittings act together to form a security system aimed at preventing or discouraging forced entry.

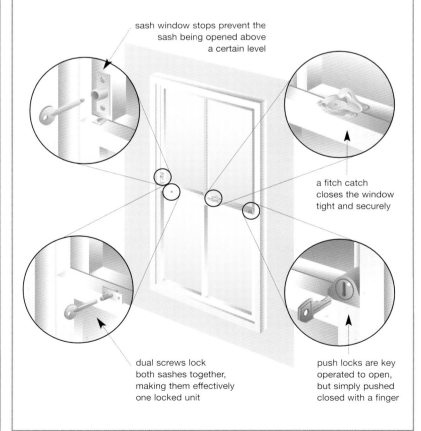

sash window stops prevent the sash being opened above a certain level

a fitch catch closes the window tight and securely

dual screws lock both sashes together, making them effectively one locked unit

push locks are key operated to open, but simply pushed closed with a finger

insulating windows

The most effective form of window insulation is clearly to choose the pvc option and have new window units installed. In many cases, however, this can prove too expensive and other ideas need to be considered when looking at the best way of improving insulation in your home. Fitting a further window layer or insulatory barrier to an existing window offers a cheaper form of insulation than full double glazing, and is therefore often referred to as secondary double glazing.

fitting secondary double glazing – sliding doors

Sliding secondary double glazing tends to be fitted in window recesses, and its design still allows access to the main window so that it may be opened and closed as required. These units tend to be supplied in a kit form by manufacturers, which is then cut to size and fitted to your particular requirements.

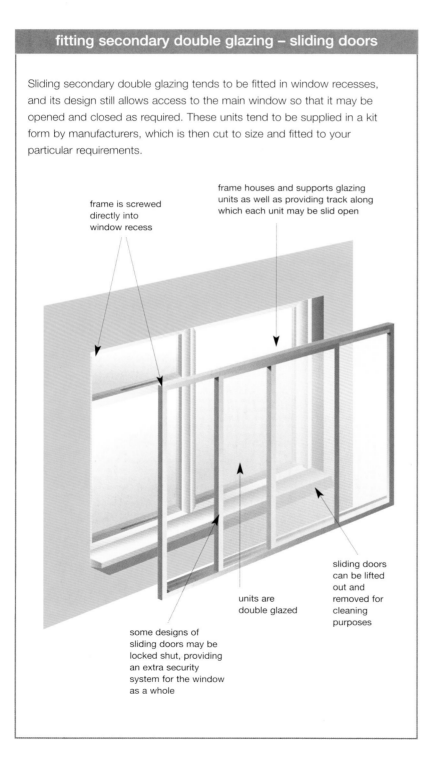

frame is screwed directly into window recess

frame houses and supports glazing units as well as providing track along which each unit may be slid open

units are double glazed

sliding doors can be lifted out and removed for cleaning purposes

some designs of sliding doors may be locked shut, providing an extra security system for the window as a whole

OTHER INSULATION OPTIONS

• **Polythene sheets** – One of the most economical ways of providing insulation is to use thin polythene sheeting, secured across the window or recess. This can be bought in kit form, and the sheet is initially secured around the window frame with tape. A hairdryer is then directed at the sheet which tautens the polythene and provides an insulatory barrier. The obvious drawback is that it is not possible to get to the window without breaking the sheet of polythene, but as a seasonal option or for windows that are rarely opened or simply do not open, this easy method is ideal.

• **Double glazed panes** – On existing wooden windows, insulation may be improved by replacing the panes of glass with double glazed units. Since these units are much thicker than normal panes, it is important first of all to check that the rebates of the windows are large enough to house the panes.

• **Draught excluders** – A further, very economical option for existing windows is to use one of the many freely available designs of draught excluder strips. Different manufacturers provide different products and designs. The two most common systems are either self-adhesive foam-based strips or more substantial plastic brush strips. The latter are mitred at the corners of the frame and fixed in place using panel pins. Different designs are suited to different types of windows.

A simpler system than the sliding doors can be found by using single pvc sheets fixed across the entire window surface. This provides an effective insulatory system, which is much simpler to fit than the sliding door mechanism shown opposite. Access is also possible in terms of opening windows if required. This is a cost effective and simple option that can either be applied on a seasonal basis or on windows which do not require frequent opening.

tools for the job

tape measure
mini hacksaw
craft knife
screwdriver

1 Accurately measure the dimensions of the entire window frame, as these will form the measurements for the plastic retaining track used to hold the pvc sheet in place. In this instance the sheet is being fitted directly onto the window frame inside the recess, but it may also be fitted on the wall surface outside, thus covering the whole recess. Prior to fitting the secondary double glazing, it is worthwhile cleaning the window on the inside and outside as access is more limited once the secondary glazing sheet is positioned.

2 Cut the track to size with a mini hacksaw or craft knife, mitring the ends to form neat joins in each corner of the window. Remove the backing of the adhesive tape on the back of the track.

3 Press the track firmly in position on the window frame, ensuring good contact between the tape and frame surface. There is normally a short period of time before the adhesive secures the track permanently in position, so minor movements or adjustments should be made quickly.

4 Once the track is in position all around the frame, lever it open. A screwdriver may be needed to help open up the track initially, but once it has begun to open it can normally be finished by hand. Measure the exact dimensions of width and height required for the pvc glazing sheet.

Transfer the measurements onto the sheet and use a mini hacksaw to cut it to size.

5 Insert the glazing sheet into the retaining track, sliding it carefully into position. Again, it is worth cleaning the sheet before positioning it, as access is limited to the inside face once it is fixed in place.

6 Finally, snap the retaining track closed onto the pvc surface, creating an effective form of insulation.

decorative finishes

All windows and doors require a decorative finish of some nature, and this is generally supplied by paint or natural wood finishes such as stain or varnish. Pvc windows and doors are normally the only exception to this rule, but manufacturers even provide systems for painting pvc once it has begun to lose its sheen and characteristic finish. In particular, windows provide an unusual example for decorative consideration, for their interior and exterior surfaces may be given similar or totally different treatment. This notion extends to exterior doors, and to a certain extent interior ones, as the decoration of one side of a door may be totally different to the other side. This chapter considers the various systems available, as well as explaining the correct and most effective methods of preparation in order to produce the best possible finished product.

Panel doors offer more surfaces for decoration and so can be incorporated into the colour scheme of a room.

choosing options

Provided the correct system is used for the window or door, colours and finishes are a matter of taste. One determining factor will be whether new replacements or existing windows and doors are being re-decorated. Replacements offer greater flexibility, since untreated wood provides a sound base for both paint and natural wood finishes, whereas you may prefer just to repaint existing windows and doors to avoid the lengthy stripping needed to achieve a natural finish.

external doors

Hardwood front doors, in particular, benefit from a natural wood system when decorated. Although paint may be used, stains are far more successful in terms of adhesion and longevity of finish. Paint is better suited to softwood doors, although stains and varnish may still be used to provide a long-lasting and durable finish. Remember that external doors provide a focal point for the house exterior, and it is therefore important to produce as good quality a finish as possible in order to show off these features of house design. Careful attention must also be given to using the correct paint or natural wood systems and applying these following the correct order of work.

RIGHT *The front door of your home often provides a first impression of the house as a whole. Ensure decoration is of the highest possible standard.*

internal doors

Internal doors clearly do not suffer from attack from the elements like their external counterparts, so considerations can defer entirely to those of taste and preference. Choosing colours or finishes that complement the surrounding decor tends to have the most beneficial effect on the room as a whole. Remember that doors come in for close scrutiny because they are viewed at close quarters when entering or leaving a room, and therefore taking time to achieve a good finish is vital for producing an attractive and professional look to the room as a whole. Also consider that it can be effective to alter the door finish rather than features in a room.

LEFT *Panel doors provide a more ornate finish than flush doors and allow for experimentation in colour scheming.*

stained windows

Wood stain will help to show off the naturally attractive qualities of wood grain and features, and vast colour ranges mean that lighter softwoods may be stained to mimic the colours of more exclusive hardwood options. Another thing to consider is that stains and varnishes do not tend to decay in the same flaky and destructive manner as paint.

painted windows

In many instances, painted windows provide the best option for decoration, especially when re-decorating previously painted ones or simply as a matter of preference to complement the other facets of house design and look. Colour choice is vast and decisions may therefore be geared towards blending with other decorative features.

ABOVE *The natural wood finish of this arch window adds to an already relaxed and airy atmosphere.*

RIGHT *Sash windows provide easy elegance in a room design which may be embellished by extravagant window dressings.*

BELOW *The old-fashioned, rustic style of the door suits this traditional room, whilst contrasting wood finishes add interest.*

combining finishes

There is no hard and fast rule which dictates that windows and doors must be given the same finish, and in many cases a pleasant effect can be achieved by combining finishes to create a more interesting decorative scheme of contrasting effects. It is often the case that doors are given a natural wood finish whilst the rest of the woodwork in a room is painted to contrast with this look.

choosing materials

Materials should clearly be chosen with quality in mind and, to a certain extent, expense determines the quality and hardwearing properties of the paint or natural wood finish you buy. It is important to choose the correct materials for a particular surface or job, so that the right system is used to obtain the desired finished product. You also need to choose the correct tools for the job – a small toolbox of selected painting equipment is a necessity.

tools for the job

The most essential equipment for painting doors and windows is a good selection of brushes. Pure bristle brushes tend to be the most multi-purpose, whereas synthetic ones are generally better suited to water-based or acrylic finishes. Fitches are useful for fine detailed work and mini rollers may sometimes be used to cover door surfaces quickly and efficiently.

mini roller

mini roller tray

lining fitch

fitches

synthetic bristle brushes   dusting brush   paint kettle   pure bristle brushes

door and window finishes

This table contains information on the properties of most of the paints and materials required for adding protective and decorative coatings to doors and windows. Aside from these examples, there are other proprietary alternatives available which are always worth considering when decorating door and window surfaces.

type	properties and areas of use
knotter	Used to seal in sap or resin from knots in wood before further coats of paint or stain are added. Available in 'white' or darker types, with the former used for preparation prior to some natural wood finishes.
primer	Available water- or solvent based. Solvent based is best suited to exterior woodwork, whilst water-based alternatives have a short drying time.
undercoat	Water- or solvent based and used as the intermediary paint coat between primers and top finishing coats, such as gloss or eggshell.
oil-based eggshell	Can be used on interior door and window surfaces, but not ideal for exterior use. Matt finish. Very hardwearing and covers well. Long drying time between coats.
acrylic or water-based eggshell	Can be used on doors or windows, easier to apply than oil-based equivalents. Slightly higher sheen than oil-based eggshell. Hardwearing, and short drying time allows for a quick finish.
gloss	Available in water- or oil-based forms. Best suited to woodwork which has been correctly primed and undercoated. Very hardwearing. Long drying time, especially for oil-based varieties.
wood stain	Water or solvent based, providing a translucent coloured finish to bare wood. Sometimes requires knotting prior to application. Normally 2–3 coats required. Varying sheens from matt to gloss finish.
varnish	Hard, protective water- or oil-based finish for natural wood finishes. May be applied direct to bare wood or over the top of stain as a further protective coating. Matt to high gloss finishes available.
Scandinavian oil	Another natural wood finish which is best suited to hardwoods. May be used inside or out. Deep penetrating protection, providing a medium sheen when polished.

The order of work or application for different systems must be adhered to so that the correct and most durable finish is achieved. Systems may again be divided into interior and exterior situations, and whether paint or a natural wood finish is used. Paint systems can vary so always check guidelines before applying coats.

interior wood water-based paint system

white knotter – used for most water-based systems, although dark knotter may sometimes be used

primer – first coat of primer undercoat applied

undercoat – provides base for top coat

top coat – eggshell or gloss, providing finished look

interior wood solvent-based paint system

dark knotter – generally more resilient than white knotter

primer – deep penetrating into wood surface

undercoat – applied as base for top coat

top coat – eggshell or gloss, providing finished look

exterior wood solvent-based paint system

dark knotter – hardwearing

preservative primer – watery consistency which penetrates deep into wood

undercoat – first undercoat

second undercoat – extends hardwearing properties of finish

top coat – provides finished look and is very hardwearing compared to interior

exterior wood stain system

white knotter – should be applied if listed in manufacturer's guidelines

first coat stain – often slightly diluted to act as primer

second coat stain – provides base coat for top coat

top coat stain – provides finish

preparing windows & doors ↗

However well a door or window is painted, the finish will deteriorate quickly unless the right amount of preparation has been given to the particular surface. The degree of preparation will also depend on whether the wood has been previously coated or whether you are starting from a completely new surface. Whatever the case, correct preparation is a vital part of ensuring the best finish possible and is an area of door and window renovation that should never be skipped over.

decorative finishes

tools for the job

| paintbrush |
| knotting brush or fitch |
| scraper |
| sealant gun |
| filling knife |

new wood

The correct order of work on new wooden surfaces was shown on page 103 but not the necessary guidelines on technique, and it is very important to have a sound appreciation of how to deal with new wood surfaces.

1 All new wood requires thorough sanding before decorative coats are applied. The grade of sandpaper you use will depend on the roughness of the surface, but in general a medium to fine grade of paper is ideal for most 'prepared' wood surfaces. Always remember to sand in the same direction as the wood grain – this is especially important if natural wood finishes are to be applied.

2 Once sanded, the wooden surface must be wiped to remove any dust or sanding residue. Failure to do this will simply cause such debris to become part of the first decorative coating layer, leaving a gritty or semi-rough surface. A cloth dampened in white spirit is ideal as it picks up the dust while cleaning the surface. White spirit also evaporates quickly allowing decorative coats to be applied soon after cleaning.

3 If the surface is to be painted, knotting solution must be applied to all the knots prior to priming. There is often a brush built into the lids of pots of knotting solution. If this is not the case

tips of the trade

Whether wood is old or new, it is likely that some filling will be required in order to achieve the best finish. All-purpose filler is best for holes in flat surfaces as it may be sanded. Caulk is best for cracks or joints as its flexible formulation will help tolerate future movement along joints and so avoid future cracking.

with the brand you are using, simply apply the solution with a fitch, ensuring that all knots are treated. It is always advisable to apply two coats of solution to each knot so you are sure it is properly covered.

4 Once the knotter or knotting solution has dried, the wood may now be primed. Work the primer into the wooden surface, spreading and brushing it out, avoiding drips or runs. Once the primer is applied and has dried, give the surface a light sand with fine grade sandpaper, and clean down with white spirit once more as described in step 2. Undercoats and top coats may then be added as required.

previously coated wood

For wood that has been previously decorated and therefore has existing decorative coatings already on it, systems need to be varied slightly. Initial attention must be turned to preparing the surface, or making good for re-decoration.

1 Sand the surface thoroughly – a coarser grade sandpaper than for new wood will often be required to remove any lumps and bumps in a painted surface, returning it to a smoother base for re-decoration.

2 The edge of a scraper is also useful to remove any flaky material from the surface, and especially to rake out cracks in wooden joints where loose flakes of paint tend to occur.

3 Along the raked-out joints and cracks, apply a bead of decorator's caulk using a sealant gun. Take care not to apply too much as excess will be wasted – just use enough caulk to comfortably fill the joint neatly and effectively.

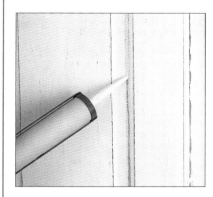

4 Run a wetted finger over the caulked joint to smooth its surface in readiness for painting. Caulk must be smoothed before it dries, as it cannot be sanded like all-purpose filler.

5 All-purpose filler should be applied to any dents, scrapes or holes in the wooden surface. This should be allowed to dry and sanded to a smooth finish before applying decorative coatings.

FURTHER POINTS TO NOTE

• **Patch priming** – On previously painted wood, some surfaces may have disintegrated back to bare wood. Where this happens, apply primer to these areas before continuing with further coats of paint.

• **Natural wood** – Preparation and fillers used in natural wood finishes differ from those for painted surfaces, since the translucent nature of oils and stains means that traditional caulks and all-purpose fillers will be visible. It is therefore necessary to use proprietary fillers that are designed for natural wood finishes such as stain and varnish. Likewise, the type of knotting solution used in some natural wood systems must be 'white' so that it is not visible through the finishing coats (as shown on page 103).

• **Exterior extras** – Preparation for exterior windows and doors tends to be more extensive than for interior work, as outside wood will have come under attack from the elements and deterioration can be very severe. This generally means that sanding and filling take longer, and putty may need replacing in some areas.

• **Stripping wood** – Many experts used to recommend stripping back to the bare wood before re-decoration. This is still necessary if you wish to change a painted surface into a natural wood finish. Otherwise, there is no call for the extreme measure of using heat guns or chemical strippers. The quality of today's decorative coatings means that old painted surfaces may be painted over to good effect, and most natural wood finishes are designed so that 'refresher' or 'maintenance' coats can be applied over previously coated surfaces. If you have to choose the total stripping option, always obey the appropriate safety guidelines for handling potentially dangerous heat guns and chemical strippers.

painting techniques – 1 ⚒

Quite simply, there is a right and a wrong way to paint any item, and doors are no exception – you must refine your technique so that the best possible quality of finish is achieved. Once preparation and priming has been completed, application of undercoats and finishing coats follows the same system or order of work. Doors vary in design, but one of the more common varieties is the panel door, and the best way of achieving a good finish is demonstrated below.

tools for the job

375mm (1½in) paintbrush
250mm (1in) paintbrush

painting a panel door

Panel doors vary in design from two large panels making up their surface, to as many as eight panels. However, the best system for painting them stays the same and here a six-panelled door has been used. Choice of brush size is very important, and a 375mm (1½in) brush is ideal in most cases.

1 Begin by painting the panels themselves, starting at the top. As well as painting the central flat area of the panel, also complete the moulded area and try not to allow paint to encroach onto the rails or stiles.

2 Continue to work down the door, completing all the panels, using the bristles of the brush in line with the direction of the wood grain. Even if you are painting a pressed

panel door which does not have any 'grain' as such, still direct the brush in the direction of what would be the perceived grain.

3 Once the panels are complete, move on to paint the central vertical stiles down the middle of the door. Try not to allow the paint to extend on to the horizontal rails, and if any excess encroaches on the painted panels, ensure that you brush the paint out to prevent a paint build-up.

4 Move on to coat the horizontal rails to complete the central portion of the door. Take care when creating the join between these rails and the painted vertical stiles to

ensure a precise defining line. This will maintain the principle of painting in line with the grain and therefore provides the neatest possible finish.

5 Finish the face of the door by painting the two outer vertical stiles on the hinge and opening edge of the door. Again, make precise divisions at the point where the vertical stiles cross the edges of the horizontal rails whilst still brushing the paint out in the usual manner.

6 Paint the leading edge of the door using a 250mm (1in) brush to avoid overspray. Take care to paint precisely down the edge of the door only and not on the door face.

7 Now that the door itself is complete, turn your attention to the door architrave. The hinge edge of the door in this instance need not be painted as it should be the same colour as the other face of the door. Begin on the architrave by painting the edge.

8 With the architrave edges complete, paint the face of the mouldings, returning to the 375mm (1½in) brush for quicker coverage.

9 Paint the inner door stop and remaining side of the frame, and check for any areas that you have missed. Finally, turn attention back to

the face of the door to make sure there are no drips on the paint surface. 'Brush in' such areas as required.

flush doors

Flush doors do not have the complicated surface of panel doors.

Hence they may be treated more as an overall open surface, which is best painted by mentally dividing the door area into eight equal-sized sections, beginning with two at the top and three further rows of two areas as you go down the door surface. It is important to maintain a 'wet edge' in the paint as you move from each area to the next, so that there is no visible join between each of the eight areas. The architrave and door frame may be painted as for panel doors.

glazed doors

When painting a glazed door it should be treated more like a casement window than a solid door surface.

A well painted door forms an integral part of any room decoration. Attention to detail and precise dividing lines help to enhance its look and provide a good quality finish.

painting techniques – 2

In a similar manner to doors, to achieve the best possible finish for windows it is necessary to follow a particular order of work. But accuracy is even more important as it is vital to prevent paint transference or overspray reaching any glass surface. Therefore, as we have seen is the case with doors, windows must be 'broken down' into different sections and painted systematically, according to the order listed below.

tools for the job

250mm (1in) paintbrush

casement windows

Casement windows provide a good example of how all window painting should be approached. Casements themselves vary in design, with different types and sizes of opening section, but a similar principle regarding the order of work applies. Remember to look back continually to painted areas and brush out any drips or runs that you find before the paint dries. Make sure that you pay particular attention to the numerous joints and corners, which provide areas where paint could build up.

1 Initially, attention should be aimed towards the smallest opening casement. Begin by painting the rebates using a 25mm (1in) brush. Take care to bead the paint directly along the rebate/glass junction, creating a precise edge.

tips of the trade

• **Preparing the sill** – Before painting a windowsill, wipe over it with a cloth dampened in white spirit and allow to dry before applying paint. This removes dust particles and improves the overall finish.

• **Window guards** – If you find producing a precise edge between rebate and glass particularly difficult, it may be worth using a window guard. These specially designed pieces of metal or plastic can be held along the junction of glass and wood, positioned to shield the glass surface so that paint is applied only to the wood. However, after painting each rebate, the edge of the window guard or shield should be cleaned with a cloth to remove excess paint, and prevent it being transferred to the glass surface when it is next positioned.

• **Drying time** – Always allow sufficient drying time for paint. Closing the window too early will almost certainly lead to it sticking shut.

2 Move on to complete the rest of the small opening casement, first painting the horizontal rails, and then the vertical ones. Remember always to keep the brush bristles in line with the direction of the wood

grain, depending on which section of the casement is being painted. This creates a neat finish between vertical and horizontal rails.

3 Now move on to the larger opening casement, beginning once again with the window rebates. Start painting the top panes and work down the window rebates to the bottom level of the pane.

4 You can now finish painting the opening casement by completing the central horizontal and vertical rails. The very last parts that are left to be painted are the outer vertical rails on the hinged side and the leading edge of the casement.

5 Then paint the fixed casements, starting on the rebates first before finishing with the open faces of the rails.

6 Next, paint around the internal rebates of the main window frame, between the outer edge of the frame and the casements themselves. When working next to the opening casements, be sure to paint a precise dividing line so that there is no untidy overspill on the window edges.

7 Finally, complete the main face of the window by painting the outer frame. Similar accuracy is required here for painting the rebates

next to the glass. Always produce a precise dividing line between the window frame and the wall surface.

8 With the window complete, the sill may be painted to provide the overall finished product.

It is worth noting that painting the exterior of a window is very similar to the interior, except the rebates may be putty or wood. The technique used will remain very much the same.

sash windows

Painting sash windows follows similar principles as for casements, starting next to the glass and working out towards the frame being the best method. The main problem with sashes is when painting the runners, as this tends to be the area where sticking may occur and hinder the mechanism of the window. It is therefore worth inspecting the runners closely before beginning to paint – if they do not require re-coating, then it is not worth painting them purely for the sake of it. Bear in mind that the runners are obscured most of the time, and it is better to have them functioning easily than stuck fast because of layers of paint build-up. From an aesthetic point of view as well, efforts should be concentrated on window parts that are most visible.

A well painted window provides clean, crisp lines which show good attention to detail, enhancing the overall look of the room decoration.

applying natural wood finishes

Natural wood finishes differ from painted ones in that the latter form an opaque finished product whereas the former provide a semi-transparent or translucent finish. A top coat of colour combines nicely with the aesthetic qualities of the wood grain used in door or window make-up. As already mentioned, compared to the techniques used for paint application there are vital differences in the preparation for and application of such coatings.

Wood stain is one of the most popular forms of natural wood finish, since it is relatively easy to apply and provides an instant and sometimes dramatic finish to a wooden surface. As with all such finishes, the more prominent the wood grain the better the finished look, because the formulation of the stain is made to enhance the grain and highlight its natural beauty. Modern innovation has also meant that stains are not only available in traditional browns or wood effect shades, but in an entire range of colours as well.

1 Apply stain to surfaces using a similar order of work to paint, again following the grain, but also ensuring that the stain is well brushed out and no streaks or overlaps are left in the finished surface.

2 Particular attention must also be paid to the joints between different sections of wood, as overlaps will show through in the finished product. Use the extreme edge of the bristles on the brush to create precise dividing lines between the different sections of wood which combine to make up the door surface.

varnish

Varnish may be applied over the top of some stains for added protection, or direct to the wood, providing a finish in its own right. It is therefore best used on bare wood when the grain itself is particularly attractive or pronounced. Being, in general, completely transparent, it can be difficult with varnish to see where previous brush

tips of the trade

There are further natural wood alternatives to those mentioned, with various wood dyes available and hybrids such as stain varnish, which as the name suggests, combines the two finishes in one product. It can sometimes be worth experimenting with these products to determine their effectiveness, though you might want to test them first to ensure that they live up to their claims.

strokes have been made. This makes it doubly important to keep to a strict order of work so that you know exactly where previous strokes are. In this way, even coats will be applied.

1 Apply the varnish with the grain, taking care to brush it out thoroughly to reduce the risk of drips or runs, which look unsightly.

2 Between coats, it is advisable to sand the surface lightly to remove any rough areas, as the varnish can tend to lift the grain of the wood. With the sandpaper, apply only enough pressure to remove these rough areas. Too much pressure will score the varnished surface.

waxes

Waxes are really the most traditional of natural wood finishes and are available in many different forms, from natural products to synthetic alternatives. As with stains, there are more colour choices than in years gone by, from neutral varieties ranging to finishes of a more colourful nature. The main drawback with wax is that re-coating tends to be needed more frequently than with other natural wood coatings, but it does provide an attractive, polished wood finish.

1 Firstly, open up the grain of the wood using a wire brush. Be sure only to work in the same direction as the grain; never use the brush in a circular motion.

2 Generously apply wax – in this case a white limewax has been used – to the wooden surface. Use wire wool to rub the wax well into the wood, again working in the direction of the grain.

3 Allow the wax to dry, but not to a state where it is fully hardened off, and use a clean dry cloth to polish the surface of the wood. One or two further applications of wax may be required to provide the best finish.

oil

Oil, or what is more commonly known as Scandinavian oil, provides a similar effect to wax, but is available in fewer varieties. Its effect is to tint the wood slightly, making the most of the grain and providing it with a hardwearing and slightly polished finish.

safety advice

Scandinavian oil is highly flammable and the rags used must be disposed of in a safe manner.

1 Apply the oil with a brush, coating the wood generously whilst still brushing the oil out and

allowing it to soak into the wood. Be very careful when you do this to avoid getting any runs in the finish.

2 Immediately after application, polish the surface of the wood with a cloth, removing excess oil and buffing up the surface to a finish. This process will not produce a high sheen but more of a semi-gloss effect. Application of further coats with more buffing after each should further improve the sheen of the finish.

EXTERIOR USE

• Most natural wood finishes may be applied on both interior and exterior wood, with wax the main exception as it tends to deteriorate too quickly when applied outside.

• Oil will tend to weather quickly outside, but, although the finish deteriorates, its protective qualities are still maintained.

• Before applying stains or varnishes to exterior wood, always check the manufacturer's guidelines on the uses their product is recommended for.

• Also remember that quick-drying or water-based alternatives are available and can be advantageous for completing jobs in a day, and for use during inclement weather conditions.

• For exterior work it is worth applying an extra coat over and above the manufacturer's guidelines to enhance the wood's weathering capabilities.

repair & restoration

Doors and windows are expensive yet essential elements in the make up of your home, and therefore need to be looked after to as great a degree as possible. Normal issues of wear and tear must be addressed to understand how problems occur and what are the best techniques for repair and restoration. Many of these problems are simple and fall into the category of nothing more than general servicing to ensure that operation of doors and windows is maintained. However, other repairs may be more extensive, requiring more detailed measures when it comes to restoration. The following chapter covers a wide range of topics in this area, and helps to demonstrate the best and most suitable techniques for dealing with the most common problems likely to be experienced.

These window panes feature a water lily stained glass design that complements the bathroom function of this room.

recognizing problems

An appropriate diagnosis is the first step to addressing any problems, and because doors and windows almost always include an opening and closing function and mechanism, many of their problems relate to the various ways in which this function is either hindered or prevented. The second major consideration is that although many problems are caused by general wear and tear over time, most door and window problems occur in those that are constructed from wood.

problem areas on doors

There are a number of areas on doors where problems may occur, with some being far more serious and more difficult to fix than others. This example shows many of the areas and points where problems may occur.

door sticking at top – can be caused by one of the door hinges loosening and thus allowing the door to drop one end whilst raising on the other. The door will need to be removed and re-hung or excess planed from the top.

door sticking at sides – more often than not, this is caused by paint build-up over the years. Planing is therefore all that is required. Alternatively, it may be down to hinge movement and the door may need to be re-hung.

door sticking at bottom – normally caused by hinges dropping or, on external doors, damp penetration at the base could cause the wood to swell and expand. The door will need to be removed and re-hung or excess planed from the bottom. Alternatively, an uneven floor surface may cause this problem, and changing normal butt hinges to rising butts should clear it up.

CAUTION

• **General sticking** – Sometimes sticking doors can point to more serious problems, as wall subsidence may knock a door frame out of line, creating a misshapen aperture for the door to close into. If in any doubt, therefore, seek professional advice on this matter, but remember that this sort of problem is relatively rare and sticking doors are more likely to result from the other explanations provided.

• **Warping doors** – This can occur with relatively cheap doors soon after installation. To avoid this happening, ensure that the doors are stored flat before installation and are left in the room they are to be put in for a number of days before being hung. This enables them to get used to the prevailing atmospheric conditions.

• **Sticking latch** – Gradual movement over time, or an old door which has slowly been planed and planed to fit the frame, may eventually reach a point where planing cannot continue because the latch plate is proud of the door edge. It is therefore necessary to recess the latch plate further into the door edge.

• **Hinge bound** – Where hinges have not been recessed into the door lining and/or door edge, a situation arises where the door is unable to close onto the doorstop. As a result pressure is put upon the hinges, which may eventually cause the door lining or door edge to split or damage. Resetting the hinge position is therefore necessary.

problem areas on casement windows

Due to the fact that casement windows work on a hinge mechanism, many of their problems can be seen as similar to those suffered by doors. Sticking casements and the reasons for such occurrences are therefore often similar to those given for doors. However, windows will always have an external aspect and the diagram below illustrates some other problems that may occur.

1 damp penetration – sealant around the edge of the window can deteriorate and will need to be replaced.

2 damp penetration – drip guard is blocked so that moisture accumulates below sill and penetrates. Drip guard needs to be cleaned out or re-routed.

3 damp penetration – deterioration in putty or beads will allow water in around the edges of glass panes. Repairs required.

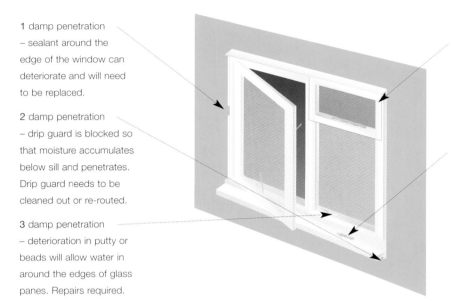

sticking casements – caused by paint build-up or swelling during damp conditions. Sometimes due to hinging problems. Normally a little planing will fix the problem, but in some cases re-hinging will be required.

rot and infestation – sometimes damp and/or insect attack can cause problems with wooden windows. If caught early enough small, localized areas can be treated, filled or partially replaced with new wood. Failure to carry out repairs quickly may lead to total window replacement being necessary.

problem areas on sash windows

Many of the problems found with sashes are the same as illustrated with casement windows. In other words, rot and damp problems are just as likely to occur. However, there are some other problems that relate specifically to sash windows, as shown in the illustration below.

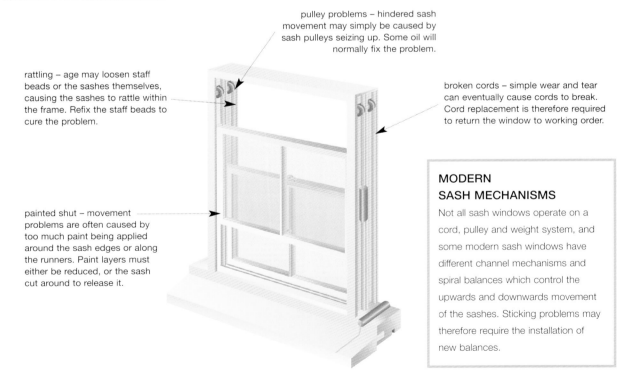

pulley problems – hindered sash movement may simply be caused by sash pulleys seizing up. Some oil will normally fix the problem.

rattling – age may loosen staff beads or the sashes themselves, causing the sashes to rattle within the frame. Refix the staff beads to cure the problem.

broken cords – simple wear and tear can eventually cause cords to break. Cord replacement is therefore required to return the window to working order.

painted shut – movement problems are often caused by too much paint being applied around the sash edges or along the runners. Paint layers must either be reduced, or the sash cut around to release it.

MODERN SASH MECHANISMS

Not all sash windows operate on a cord, pulley and weight system, and some modern sash windows have different channel mechanisms and spiral balances which control the upwards and downwards movement of the sashes. Sticking problems may therefore require the installation of new balances.

releasing sticking doors & windows ⤢

Once diagnosed, sorting out window and door sticking problems becomes a comparatively straightforward task of simply choosing the right technique to deal with the particular problem at hand. As in all instances, it is best to start by trying the easy cures before moving on to the more complicated and time-consuming ones.

simple solutions

With sticking doors, especially along the sides, it is best to begin by trying the simpler solutions before taking more dramatic action, which may entail extensive wood removal from the door edge. Sometimes slight seasonal changes in response to atmospheric conditions can cause minimal expansion and contraction of door surfaces, and minimal easing is therefore all that is required.

tools for the job

candle
sandpaper or sanding block
wood plane
jigsaw
craft knife

1 Rub a candle down the leading edge of the door. Sometimes, this small transference of wax onto the

door edge can help to ease its operation, allowing the door to open and close more easily.

2 If this does not work, use some sandpaper or a sanding block down the edge. Start on the rough side and progress to the smooth side.

3 If still more easing is required, resort to using a wood plane and gradually shave off sections of wood along the door edge. Take care not to work all along the door edge as it may only be sticking in one localized area. It is normally possible to see

where the door is sticking by closing it and making a mark with a pencil to show where the obstructing areas are.

4 Set the plane so that only small amounts of wood are shaved off each time. Keep opening and closing the door to monitor the situation until ease of function is restored. The door edge may then be repainted.

👍 tips of the trade

In some circumstances, paint build-up on a door edge must be reduced to help the opening and closing mechanism of the door. A heat gun can be used to remove excess paint initially, before employing a wood plane to smooth the surface. Paint may otherwise clog up the workings and blade of the plane, making it difficult to move along the door edge, so removal of the paint first is a good option. Remember when using heat guns to adhere to all safety rules and guidelines, and never to leave a heat gun unattended when switched on.

bottom of door sticking

When a door is sticking at the bottom it is best to use a scribing technique to measure how much wood needs to be removed in order to ease movement.

Put the door in a closed position. Cut a block of wood with a height representing the required clearance between the bottom of the door and the floor. Hold a pencil tight on top of the block, with its point resting on the block edge. Draw the block and pencil across the floor surface at the base of the door, leaving a pencil guideline along the bottom of the door. The door may now be removed from its hinges and trimmed to this guideline. For small cuts a wood plane may be used. For larger sections, a jigsaw is the ideal tool. Re-hang the door once the wood has been removed.

sash sticking

Sticking sashes is a common problem, and before attempting to take any mechanisms apart it is worth checking whether the window has simply been 'painted shut'.

If a window has been painted without allowing any movement of the sashes, it is likely that as the paint dries it will form a bond between the sashes and runners and therefore prevent the window from being opened. To cure this situation, simply use a craft knife to run around the edge of the sash, thus breaking the bond or seal and freeing up the window so that it may freely be moved up and down once more.

On occasion, the door furniture itself may be responsible for preventing doors from opening and closing easily. This is usually due to the latch mechanism sitting proud of the door edge and catching the door frame or catch plate as it closes.

tools for the job

screwdriver

chisel

1 Remove the door handles and unscrew the latch plate. With some latches this may be a two-stage process, with a second cover plate actually covering the main latch.

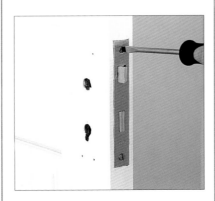

2 It can be tricky to pull the latch out of the door, for if it has been fitted correctly it should be held tightly. Therefore position a screwdriver where the door handle spindle would

normally be, and pull on both the handle and the shaft of the screwdriver simultaneously, to pop the latch out from its recessed position.

3 Once out, use a sharp chisel to remove more wood from the recess, gradually scraping the recess surface back and taking care not to remove too much wood. If a lot of wood removal is required, you will need to reposition the hole for the handle and lock, as any adjustment in latch plate position will push the handle position away from the door edge and across the door surface.

4 Once you are happy with the amount of wood removed, replace the latch and check that the door closes before fixing it back in place. Remember that because the handle is not yet in position, once the door is shut it will not be possible to open it unless you have a flat-head screwdriver available to insert into the latch and act as a temporary handle, whilst you check the door opening and closing function.

fixing loose doors & windows

As well as the common irritants relating to sticking doors or windows, there are also problems of equal inconvenience when doors or windows are loose and do not function properly. Whereas sticking problems tend to require removal of wood or recessing of fittings, 'loose' ones require the opposite remedy, with an addition of material needed to restore function.

adjusting a catch plate

As explained below, addition of wood strips is an extreme measure, and, for a door that is loose, a simpler solution is to adjust the position of the catch plate. Bringing the plate fractionally away from the door frame is usually all that is needed to allow the latch to hold in position once the door is shut.

ADDING WOOD

Where there is a huge difference between the width of a door and its frame, there is clearly a need to actually add wood to the edges of the door. This situation may only arise in extreme circumstances, or where a door that is obviously too narrow is moved to fit into a wider frame. In these cases, it literally becomes a procedure of cutting strips to the depth and width requirement, and screwing them to the door edges. It may be necessary to screw strips to both edges to maintain the balanced look of the door, especially if it is a panelled design. For smaller additions, joining on one side may be all that is required. If attempting this technique, remember that accuracy is vital in order to keep joins unnoticeable, and it is likely that the door will require a painted finish, because a natural wood coating may highlight the joined strips and make the repair too obvious.

tools for the job

screwdriver

scissors

craft knife

1 Unscrew the catch plate from its fixed position. It may require a little persuasion by levering it free with the end of a flat-head screwdriver.

2 On a piece of card, draw a pencil guideline around the edge of the catch plate itself.

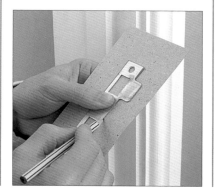

3 Cut out the catch plate template precisely using scissors, but do not worry about cutting away the extended front section as this is an area which is not required when you fit the card in the recess itself.

4 Position the cardboard template in the catch plate recess, trimming as necessary to make any final adjustments for fitting precisely and tightly in place.

5 Screw the catch plate back in place, through the template and into the screw fixing holes below.

6 Use a craft knife to cut out the holes for housing the latch and lock. Try closing the door to see if the movement of the plate has affected the closed position. If the door is still loose, remove the catch plate and add a further piece of card to increase the 'packing'. Continue to add and test until the door closes properly.

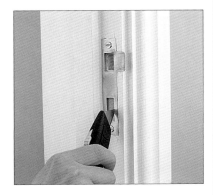

rattling doors

Rattling doors provide another example of how a door may be loose fitting, but in this case the door itself may be a perfect fit in terms of its position in the frame, with the actual problem relating to the position of the doorstop. In other words, the doorstop has been positioned too far from the latch, so that even small gusts of wind or draughts cause the door latch to rattle rather than being held firmly in place by the latch position and doorstop combined. Conversely, the door may not close properly, because the doorstop is positioned too far forward or too close to the catch plate, and therefore the door cannot physically be shut in place. The remedy for this problem is fortunately very simple.

tools for the job

old chisel
pencil
hammer

1 Remove the doorstop by carefully levering it out of position using an old chisel to assist you.

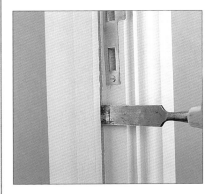

2 Close the door and mark a line on the door lining to show where the ideal position for the edge of the doorstop will be, to allow the door to close tightly but still easily. Simply reopen the door and nail the doorstop back in place according to the new guidelines.

It may also be necessary to move the doorstop on the head and hinged side of the frame, so check for this once the first piece of doorstop has been repositioned.

loose casements

The opening casements in windows may also rattle or become loose, often as a result of them warping slightly or losing shape through age and weather attack. This situation may often be helped by adjusting the window closing mechanism and more specifically the position of the window

stays. The fixing plate of a window stay is usually positioned closer to the hinging edge of the casement than the opening edge. This allows the window to be opened further. However, where a window has warped, by moving the fixing plate closer to the opening edge greater leverage is gained when closing the window and therefore the stay helps to pull the casement back into shape.

tools for the job

screwdriver
bradawl or pencil
cordless drill/driver

1 Simply unscrew the stay fixing plate from its position near the hinged edge of the casement.

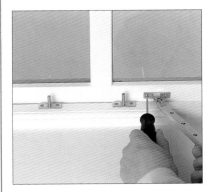

2 Reposition it, using a bradawl or pencil to mark the new fixing position. Pilot drill holes and screw the stay in place. There is normally no need to reposition the stay pins.

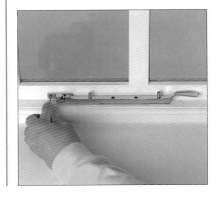

repairing hinges 🔨🔨🔨

Many of the problems associated with doors and windows failing to open and close efficiently are caused by faulty hinging mechanisms, such as hinges not positioned correctly or not working in the appropriate manner. Outlined here are some common remedies for malfunctioning hinges on both doors, as shown, and casement windows.

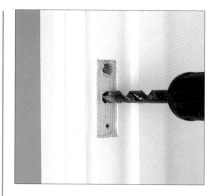

tools for the job

hammer
craft knife
screwdriver
cordless drill/driver
wooden mallet
chisel
pencil
scissors
saw
wood plane

loosening stubborn screws

When dealing with hinge problems, the first obstacle to overcome can in fact be removing the screws from their position. When hinges have not been painted removal tends to be relatively simple, but for painted ones the process can be much more difficult.

1 Begin by using the head of a flat-head screwdriver to scrape out paint from the slot in the screw head. A craft knife may also be used here.

2 As further encouragement to moving the screws, give each one a few taps with a hammer on the screwdriver to dislodge it fractionally from its painted solid position. If the screw head is too corroded to make undoing possible, it may simply be necessary to drill out the screw and use a new fixing.

strengthening a hinge fixing

Through general wear and tear, hinges can become worn and their fixings can loosen, which results in a door moving out of position in its frame. Re-tightening screws may fix this situation, but normally the holes have become too enlarged for the screws to bite firmly. It is therefore necessary to fill the holes and redrill the fixings.

1 Remove the door from the frame. Make the existing screw holes much larger by using a large drill bit to bore into the door lining at each screw position. The size of the drilll bit should be similar to that of the diameter of the wooden dowel which will be inserted into the holes.

2 Insert lengths of wooden dowel into the bored holes, ensuring that the dowel is a tight fit. Apply some wood glue around the dowel before putting it in position.

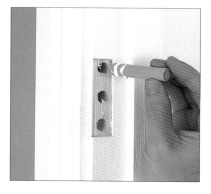

3 Knock the dowels in place using a wooden mallet, tapping carefully until the dowel extends a good distance into the hole. Avoid using a hammer for this process as it is likely to split the dowel. Use a cloth to wipe away any excess wood glue from around each dowel.

4 Leave the dowels to dry overnight so that they are glued firmly in position. Then, using a sharp chisel, cut off the dowel ends so that they are back flush with the surface of the door lining.

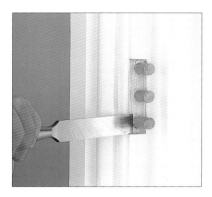

5 Holding a hinge back in position, use a pencil to mark the exact points for the screw fixings. This stage is especially important if you have changed or renewed the door hinges.

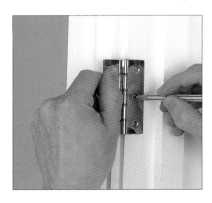

6 Using a fine bit, drill some pilot holes at each newly marked position. Finally, reposition the hinges and re-hang the door.

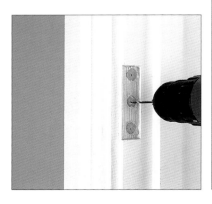

In a similar way to packing out a catch plate as shown on page 118, hinges may also be packed out to adjust the door position to close more efficiently. Instead of introducing a card template behind the catch plate, the hinges are removed and cardboard is positioned behind them.

1 Remove the door and hinges and cut some thick card to the size of the hinge recess. Be as accurate as possible with the card size to ensure that it fits snugly into the hinge recess. Try adding different thicknesses of card to aid this process. As an alternative to card, thin plyboard may also be used.

2 Position the card in the recess before screwing the hinges and door back in position. Test the door to see if closing has improved. If not, add more packing as required. You may find that the other hinge on the door will also require packing out.

For many reasons a door may be removed from an entrance, or the side it hinges on the frame may be changed. Whatever the reason, the recesses of the old hinges in the door frame need to be repaired so that the frame may be redecorated. This is achieved by a simple patching technique that fills the recess and repairs the frame.

1 Having removed the hinge and cleaned up the hole with a chisel, cut a piece of softwood down to as close to the dimensions of the hinge recess as possible. Test it fits before applying some wood glue to it and positioning it in the frame.

2 Once the glue has dried, use a wood plane to smooth the surface of the patch and bring it flush with the surrounding door frame. Finally, some fine filling may be required before repainting the area to blend in with the rest of the frame.

repairing hinges

renovating sash windows – 1

The opening mechanism of sash windows has traditionally been based on a cord, pulley and weight system, which balances the weight of the window as it is moved up and down for opening and closing purposes. When it comes to renovating and repairing these mechanisms, the process is fairly complex in the number of stages required but relatively simple to do if tasks are undertaken in the right order. The most common form of damage involves a broken sash cord.

removing the sash & replacing the cord

The balance of a sash window is such that the frame really only acts as a guide for moving the sashes. The sashes themselves are free running, using the pulley and cord mechanism as its only attachment to the frame as a whole. In other words, there is no solid or hinged attachment between a sash and the frame. However, releasing them from their operating position can be tricky.

tools for the job

old chisel or screwdriver

hammer

1 Lever away the staff bead from the main part of the frame using an old chisel or screwdriver. The bead is normally pinned in position with relatively small nails, so by moving the position of the chisel up and down the junction, gradually the fixings are loosened and the bead removed. It is

important to try not to damage the bead as it will be repositioned once the window repair is complete.

2 Remove the cover that hides the weights inside the frame of the window. These are sometimes metal plates that unscrew, but in this case the cover is made from a wooden panel. Again, use an old chisel or screwdriver to lever and ease the cover out of the frame.

3 Pull the top of the weight out from inside the frame and remove the broken section of sash cord. In some cases it may be necessary to reach right down inside the frame to locate the weight.

4 Remove the sash from the frame, remembering that when you pull the side of the sash (with the damaged cord) away from the frame, the other side of the sash will still be attached to the frame. It can thus be tricky to move the sash into a position that is clear from the frame and allows access for repairs. It is best to manoeuvre the undamaged cord so that the sash can be rested on a workbench in front of the window.

5 With the sash out of the way, this is a good opportunity to service the pulley and confirm that it is in good working order. Apply some oil to the pulley mechanism to ensure its moving parts are lubricated.

6 Take a piece of string and tie it onto a nail. Instead of using a straight nail, ensure that the one you use is slightly curved. This can be achieved with a few hammer blows.

7 Holding the untied end of the string with one hand, thread the end with the curved nail over the pulley. If the nail does not go through on the first attempt – as it is still too straight – simply increase the curve of the nail until it threads through easily.

NEW SASH SYSTEMS

Sash window design has been varied slightly in modern times with the introduction of different mechanisms to balance the sashes, but the opening principle remains the same, with the sashes still sliding along runners. Modern sash windows have vinyl or pvc linings for the runners and spiral balances in place of the traditional mechanism. However, cords and weights are still the most common sash opening mechanism.

8 Once the nail appears in the hole revealed by the removal of the weight cover, turn your attention to the other end of the string and tie a new section of sash cord to it.

9 Now thread the sash cord end, whilst tied to the string, over the pulley and into the window frame. It is important that the end of the cord is trimmed, because if it is in any way frayed it will be difficult to thread over the pulley mechanism.

10 Pull on the other end of the string (the end with the nail on it), thus pulling the cord down to

the weight cover hole. Once you can grab the end of the cord, pull it out from the hole and remove the string.

11 Thread the cord into the securing hole on the weight and tie it off tightly. Weight design will vary slightly, but generally the cord must be threaded through a hole in the top of the weight, pulled through a hole in the side of the weight, tied off and then pushed back into the side hole to wedge the knot in place.

12 In some cases, if the weight is designed to drop down into the window frame, it will be necessary to tie a knot at the other end of the cord to prevent the weight pulling it over the pulley and down into the window frame, which will oblige you to start the threading process again. Make a simple knot which can be untied easily when it is time to attach this end of the cord to the sash. Alternatively, tie off the cord onto a screwdriver, which may then be positioned next to the pulley and will prevent the cord pulling through.

renovating sash windows – 2 ↗↗↗

With the sash removed and the new cord threaded over the pulley and into the frame, attention can be turned to re-attaching the sash to the cord and getting it back into a running position. Once again it is best to follow a particular order of tasks, so that the window is, in effect, re-assembled in a good running order.

tools for the job

long-nose pliers
pencil
marker pen
scissors or craft knife
hammer
sealant gun

attaching the cord and replacing the sash

It may be worth checking the running mechanism of the other part of the sash window, to ensure that the internal parting bead allows the sash to run freely. If not, re-position it while the other sash is out of its place before tackling the broken sash.

1 Remove the remaining part of the broken sash cord. The method required will depend on the exact type of sash design. In this case, a pair of long-nose pliers is

ideal to pull the old knotted section of cord out of its position in the side of the sash. If the cord is nailed or stapled, use pliers or a claw hammer to lever out any fixings.

2 Use a pencil to mark on the front of the sash (being repaired) the exact position of the cord retaining hole located on the side of the sash.

3 Reposition the sash in the frame, so that it is in its totally open position, with the top of the sash up close to the pulley

mechanism. Untie the new section of sash cord and hold it in the appropriate position, feeling the tension of the weight balance on the cord, and use a marker pen to mark on the cord next to the position of the cord retaining hole (marked in step 2).

4 Pull the sash out of its position in the frame once more and thread the cord through the top of the sash and out through the cord retaining hole, until you see the marked-off point on the cord. This task may be better suited to two people, so that one can take the weight of the sash window whilst the other threads the cord.

5 Tie a secure knot in the cord at the marked-off point and allow it to position itself inside the retaining hole. Check your measurements again before cutting off the excess cord with a pair of scissors or a craft knife, once the knot has been securely tied. Once again, two people may be required for this process with one holding the sash window whilst the other ties off and cuts the cord.

6 Reposition the repaired sash back in the frame. Ensure that the running mechanism is working correctly by opening and closing the sash a few times, checking that the movement is smooth and that the window does not jam or become hampered in the runners. It may sometimes be necessary slightly to re-adjust the sash cord length to reach optimum levels of movement.

7 Once you are happy with the smooth-running system, the weight cover can be replaced. Wooden ones often simply lever back in position and may require one or two taps with the butt end of a hammer. Take care not to damage the cover even though the fit may be tight, because making an exact replacement is a fiddly task.

8 The staff bead may now be replaced in its original position and part-nailed in. This is a suitable time to test the running of the sash in relation to all the front staff beads. If the sash has tended to rattle, for example, it may be necessary to take out and move the beads slightly closer to the sash surface. Conversely, if the sash has generally been too tight in the runners, the beads may need to be moved away from the sash by a fractional amount. The beads can now be fully nailed in.

9 Finally, refill any nail holes in the staff bead with all-purpose filler and sand to a smooth finish once the filler has dried. Run a bead of flexible filler or caulk between the bead and the frame, and smooth with a wetted finger before it dries. The window frame may now be re-decorated.

Sash windows provide both an attractive and efficient type of window, as long as the running mechanism is kept in good order so it moves freely up and down.

replacing a broken pane ⚒

Broken panes are probably the most common window problem that prevails in most households. Rectifying the situation comes down to a straightforward case of glass replacement, though the technique required for this task will be dependent on the way in which the glass pane is secured in the window. Glass is commonly held in position by wooden beads or putty, and it is replacing a pane in a puttied window that is demonstrated below.

tools for the job

hammer
hacking knife
pliers
paintbrush
putty knife
tape measure
protective gloves
goggles

broken pane in a puttied window

1 Tape up the outside of the broken pane with masking tape, keeping the tape only on the glass surface and not encroaching onto the putty or wooden frame of the window. Take care not to apply too much pressure on the glass surface and risk shattering the glass further at this preliminary stage.

2 On the inside of the broken pane, tape a folded plastic bag to the wooden rails of the window frame. Ensure a total seal around the edge of the tape, making certain that there are no gaps or holes. The bag will prevent glass splinters from being scattered inside the house when the old pane is removed.

3 From the outside of the window, use the butt end of a hammer to tap the glass pane, knocking it inwards and allowing it to break away from the rebates of the frame. Always wear protective goggles when carrying out this process to shield your eyes from any flying glass or debris.

4 Remove the largest sections of broken glass and place them in a bucket for safe disposal later. Some putty on the window rebates may also come away during this process, and should also be disposed of. Remove only the loose material by hand and leave the more secure pieces until later.

5 Use a hacking knife to scrape around the edge of the window rebates to remove any last pieces of glass and debris. If you do not have a hacking knife, a hammer and old chisel may be used to equally good effect. Remove old sprigs or pins in the rebates with a pair of pliers.

6 Remove the plastic bag and dust off the rebate to remove any debris. Seal the surface by priming all the bare wood in the rebate and on its edges. Allow this to dry before continuing. The paint seals the surface and provides a base for the putty.

7 Apply a small amount of putty around the rebate. Make sure that the putty has been well 'worked' in your hands, to mix it up and remove any lumps before application. The putty should have a similar texture to very pliable plasticine.

CHOOSING GLASS

Measuring size requirements is considered on pages 88-9, but it is also important to consider what frame the glass is being fitted into. Although the example here shows a window, a similar technique is used for doors, though the glass used in doors must be thicker, and sometimes toughened, compared to the thinner regulations pertaining to windows. So whether cutting your own glass or leaving it to a supplier, remember to choose the correct thickness for the particular replacement pane required.

8 Press the glass into position in the frame, inserting the base first and applying pressure only near the edges of the pane. Allow the edges to become well bedded into the putty, squeezing excess out onto the interior rebate.

9 Hammer a few sprigs or pins into the rebate, next to but not touching the glass surface. This prevents any possibility of the pane falling out before the putty dries. Use a piece of card to protect the glass surface from the edge of the hammer during this process.

10 Apply another putty bead around the glass/frame junction. This bead should be of more generous proportions than the first, covering the entire rebate area.

11 Use a putty knife to 'finish' the putty surface. Rest the edge of the knife on the glass on one side and rebate edge on the other. Applying a little pressure on the blade, drag the knife across the putty surface. It may take more than one run of the knife to achieve a smooth finish. Finally, trim any excess putty from the interior rebate of the pane. Allow it to dry before re-decoration.

REPLACEMENT OPTIONS

For wooden beads, you need to remove the beads and broken glass before following installation guidelines as detailed on pages 90–91. Double glazed units in wooden frames require a similar process, but in pvc windows professional advice is advisable if a pane or unit replacement is required.

restoring lead lights ⁄⁄⁄

Some windows may be composed entirely of lead lights, whilst others have sections. The technique usually involves different glass colours being used in a pattern. Repairing broken panes is undoubtedly a fiddly job, which in some cases is best left to the professionals. However, as long as there is easy access to the damaged area, it is more than possible to make the repair yourself. If possible, remove the damaged casement section first so that it can be treated on a flat surface.

repairing hairline cracks and leaking panes

Small cracks in panes are often relatively inconspicuous to the naked eye, but will become worse unless attended to. The pane can be fully replaced, but this is generally not required as weatherproof properties can be restored by simply using some silicone sealant to seal any such problem areas.

tools for the job

dusting brush

sealant gun

cloth

1 Dust out any loose material from the glass/lead junction and apply a small but continuous bead of sealant around the junction.

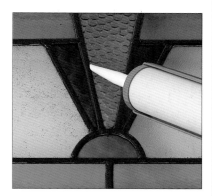

2 Use a clean cloth to remove any excess sealant from the glass surface and smooth the sealant to a finish. Turn the entire

casement over, and repeat steps 1 and 2 before repositioning the casement in the window as a whole.

replacing a broken pane

tools for the job

craft knife

chisel

goggles

putty knife

cloth

1 The method for knocking out a broken pane shown on page

126 cannot be applied to lead lights, as this will almost certainly damage the lead, and access is required right into the lead rebate. First of all, cut the putty seal between the lead and the glass, using a craft knife.

2 The pliable nature of lead allows you to fold it back away from the glass surface to reveal the glass edge. A chisel is the ideal tool for this purpose, but take care only to fold the lead back and not to cause it to tear.

3 Turn the casement over and repeat steps 1 and 2, followed by a further cut around the edge of the glass with a craft knife.

4 Turn the casement once more and tap out the broken pieces of glass. A little pressure with a cut-off piece of wood is a good tool to dislodge areas that do not come away easily. Wear protective goggles, just in case any splinters of glass are propelled from the broken pane.

5 Apply a small bead of putty around the lead rebate. Ensure that it covers the entire rebate.

6 Carefully position the new pane in the light, pressing gently to form a good contact between the glass and the putty.

7 Use the chisel to fold the lead back in place (on both sides of the casement), using the flat face of the chisel over the lead strips, moulding it back to its original finish.

8 Use a putty knife to trim away the excess putty, providing a neat finished edge to the glass/lead junction. Finally clean the glass with a clean cloth.

Lead lights, whether in doors or windows, are an attractive option for a simple casement structure. Colour variations and designs add further to the look of this finish.

renovating metal ↗↗

Restoring lead lights has been dealt with on pages 128–9, but there are many other window and door areas which display metal surfaces that at some time may require repair or renovation. Many metals are used in designs for doors and windows which are meant to be left simply with a metallic finish, such as the brass in door or window fittings.

repainting metal windows

Traditional metal windows have always required painting, but more modern versions which are normally incorporated with double glazed designs should not be painted and only require simple cleaning for restoration purposes. However, in order to obtain a satisfactory finish on metal windows that are designed for paint, it is important to follow a simple but necessary preparation procedure.

tools for the job

scraper
sanding block
wire brush
dusting brush
paintbrush

1 Remove as much flaky paint as you can from the window surface using a scraper. Applying pressure with the blade will remove much of the loose material on the rail surfaces.

The corner of the scraper blade may also be used along the joints of the window for further paint removal from these more inaccessible areas.

2 Use some rough grade sandpaper or a sanding block to smooth some more the surface of the window and further remove traces of old coats of paint.

3 For preparing metal windows, a wire brush is also useful in areas which are not flat, such as around the edge of the window casements which often demonstrate a curved profile and can render the use of a scraper ineffective.

4 Prime the bare metal with a proprietary metal primer immediately after scraping and sanding has been finished. Otherwise, exposure of the metal surface to the open air, even for a short time, may encourage corrosion of the surface to begin again. Once primed, the window may be undercoated and top coated as desired.

putty replacement

Where putty has decomposed or come loose from the glass/rebate junction, remove the affected area and replace with a new section of fresh putty. Before re-application of the putty, ensure that the window rebates are free from dust and debris and that they are primed with a metal primer. This will improve the adhesion between the putty and the window rebates. Putty should be applied using a similar technique to that for wooden windows shown on pages 126–7.

using a heat gun

The flat surfaces of metal windows are ideal for stripping using a hot air gun, and therefore this is an option or addition to the methods described above. If you do choose to use a hot air gun, remember to follow the manufacturer's guidelines and obey all safety instructions.

metal window security

As part of a general metal window renovation, it is worth introducing security systems if they are not already in place. There are proprietary locking mechanisms available for metal windows which cover both the stays and pins, and the fasteners as shown in the diagram below.

lock secured to metal frame using self-tapping screws

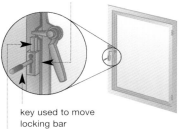

key used to move locking bar

bar locked in position below opening catch of fastener

Other proprietary systems may also be purchased to lock window stays in position. These are similar to the locking stays for wooden windows shown on page 95. Remember to keep keys in a safe place so that you have easy access in the event of an emergency. Ideally there should be a key in every room.

repainting window furniture

The window furniture on wooden windows is generally metal based. Brass fittings or those which have a 'brassed' finish should not be painted, but it can be possible to revive the look of other metal window furniture by painting it. Some fittings may have a type of paint finish on them already, and the way that a new coat of paint takes to a particular surface is variable. It can therefore be worth testing a piece of window furniture first before committing to painting it all. However, in most cases paint can be applied to these surfaces with good effect. The best method for application tends to be using aerosol paints.

tools for the job

screwdriver

wire wool

1 Always remove the window furniture from the window, and clean it down using some fine grade wire wool.

2 Place the stays and fasteners on a board, and holding the aerosol nozzle at 15–20cm (6–8in) away from the window furniture, spray it with several thin coats of paint.

3 A good way of painting the screw heads for the window furniture is to insert them in an old sponge, so that the heads point upwards, and spray them in the normal way. Once dry, all the window furniture may be refitted.

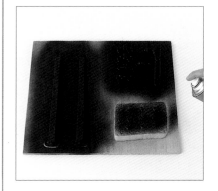

brass fittings

Many door fittings are brass or given a brass effect. For a thorough clean down it is always best to remove the particular article from the door or window, since proprietary polishes can damage the finish on other parts of the door or window surface. Always use a soft cloth when buffing up the brass to a finish.

wrought iron

Many door and window fittings are made from wrought iron and are often finished in a matt black coating. They can be revived by simple preparation and repainting. For particularly corroded pieces, immerse in an appropriate paint stripper overnight before thoroughly rinsing them down and repainting the following day.

repairing a windowsill ⁄⁄⁄

As well as being exposed to all the elements, sills come in for particular weather attack because of their function of collecting all water run-off from the window and diverting it away from the exterior walls of the house. Due to this more concentrated exposure to damp, decay is often more prevalent in sills. Unless damage is dealt with quickly, rot can spread to other parts of the window and therefore can require extensive repair or even total window replacement.

minor repairs

tools for the job

hacking knife
dusting brush and paintbrush
cordless drill/driver
protective gloves

1 Cut away loose material from the sill with a hacking knife. Give the area a clean with a dusting brush.

2 Apply a generous coating of wood hardener to the bare wood of the sill, ensuring that you

apply good coverage. Make sure to flood the area, and allow the wood to soak up the hardener.

3 Once the wood hardener has dried, mix up some wood filler and apply it to the hole concerned, making sure that it is pressed into every crevice. Wood filler is difficult to work with, and dries very quickly. It is therefore worth making more than one application, to build up layers to the level of the sill.

4 Directly adjacent to the filled area, in the sound part of the sill, drill some holes into the sill using a drill bit of equal diameter to some preservative pellets.

5 Insert the preservative pellets into the holes so that they are pushed deep into the sill. Wear protective gloves to do this as the pellets are normally very toxic so you must avoid all contact with your skin.

6 Mix up some more wood filler, and fill over the pellet holes. Once all the wood filler has dried, it may be sanded to a smooth finish and the sill repainted. Over time, the preservative pellets will break down and secrete a preservative solution into the sill. Therefore the combination of wood hardener and preservative pellets acting in tandem provide double protection against possible further wood decay.

major repairs

In some cases, sill damage becomes so extreme that the use of filler and preservatives is ineffective, and more drastic action is required.

tools for the job

old screwdriver
pencil
combination square
panel saw
cordless drill/driver
paintbrush
wood plane

1 Decide on the boundaries of the decaying area by inserting a screwdriver into the sill. If the sill is rotten, the screwdriver will penetrate the wood easily. If it is sound, the screwdriver will not break the sill surface.

2 Mark out the limits of the rotten area, extending your guideline slightly further onto the sound wood.

Draw the guideline so that the section you produce cuts into the sill at a 45 degree angle.

3 Beginning at the front of the sill, saw along the angled guideline back to the other guideline on the sill. Keep your cut as vertical as possible.

4 Saw along the back guideline to join with the other cut. The saw will usually be very close to the wall surface and this can make sawing quite difficult. Ensure that the cut is as straight as possible.

5 Use the cut-out section to mark off the replacement requirement on a new piece of prepared timber.

The timber should be of a dimension slightly larger than the cut-out section, so that once it has been fitted, it may be planed and sanded to the shape of the sill.

6 Saw down the new piece of wood to the marked-off size and pre-drill holes in the new front side of the sill. Also, use a countersink drill bit to open up the entrance point for the screws. Use wood preservative on the cut-out area on the old sill, and ensure that the new section of wood has been treated with preservative before it is fitted to the windowsill.

7 Screw the new section in place, ensuring that the screws bite deep into the existing sound section of the sill. Complete any final fitting requirements by planing the section to size. Use some wood filler to cover any joints and screw holes. More than one application of filler followed by sanding and wiping with white spirit will be required before repainting, to provide the very best finish.

refurbishing a doorway ⚒⚒⚒

Exterior doors clearly experience more punishment and wear and tear than interior doors, with much of this being due to normal weathering processes. It is therefore important to keep them in a good state of repair. Ensuring that surfaces are well decorated, and therefore preserved, is one of the best methods of preventing problems, but there are also other more structural ways in which doors may be protected.

attaching a weatherboard

Weatherboards are sloped sections of wood designed to increase run-off away from the base of an exterior door. If exterior doors do not have these fitted as part of their original design, they may be fitted later.

tools for the job

pencil
tape measure
spirit level
chisel
mallet
panel saw
cordless drill/driver
paintbrush

1 With the door in a closed position, hold a cut-off section of the weatherboard up against the door frame. Use a pencil to draw a guideline along the profile of the board and onto the hinging side of the frame. Repeat this procedure at the leading or opening edge of the

door. In each case, ensure that the base of the board is held slightly above the door threshold strip.

2 Draw a level guideline across the door, joining the top mark of each profile guideline. There may have to be some adjustment here, especially if the door is out of shape or was not hung properly. However, any adjustment must still ensure that the base of the weatherboard guideline is above the threshold strip.

3 Along each guideline on the door frame, chisel out the section of wood back to the main stiles of the frame. A small chisel is ideal for this particular job as the

size of the blade will allow you to follow the curved guideline as accurately as possible.

4 Saw the weatherboard to the length required and hold it in position, with the door still closed. Drill pilot holes through the board and into the door. Visually, it is best to place the holes in the concave part of the moulding. Five to six pilot holes should be drilled equidistantly along the weatherboard length.

5 Before fixing the weatherboard in place, paint the underside of it with a good quality primer. The priming must be done first, for once the board is fitted access to this part

of it will be impossible, and the underside is also a particularly vulnerable area for damp attack.

6 Once dry, reposition the board and fix it in place. Ensure that each pilot hole has been countersunk so that when screws are inserted, their heads will sit below the surface level of the moulding. The holes may then be filled and sanded before painting. Check the action of the door as you may need to shave a bit of wood off the leading edge of the weatherboard, so that it opens and closes smoothly into the frame.

frame problems

tools for the job

tape measure
pencil
panel saw
wrecking bar
paintbrush
cordless drill/driver
hammer

Many decay problems on exterior doors tend to occur more often in the frames than in the doors themselves. This is normally caused by damp penetration, which spreads up through the main body. It then becomes necessary to cut out the affected area and replace it with a new section of wood.

1 Determine how far the rot has progressed up the frame and make a diagonal cut slightly further along, into a sound section of wood.

2 It is likely that the section of frame to be discarded is held in position with frame fixings, and so a wrecking bar may be required to lever the section free.

3 Use the old section as a template to draw a guideline on a new piece of wood of equal dimensions to that of the door frame. Ensure that the new wood has been well treated with preservative.

4 Saw the section to the correct size and position it in the frame. Pilot hole some fixing points, ensuring that at least one fixing will penetrate through the diagonal join made by the new section and old part of the frame.

5 Screw the new section in place – concrete anchor screws have been used in this case, but it is possible to use standard frame fixings with a wall plug.

6 Cut to size and refit the missing section of doorstop. Pin this in place with nails. Fill, sand and prime the entire section before repainting.

glossary

Acrylic - or water based. Term used when referring to the make up of paint or glaze.

Angle bead - right-angled metal strip used to create a sharp profile for external corners before plaster is applied.

Architrave - decorative wooden surround applied around door frames or entrances to create finish.

Butt - alternative name for hinge.

Casement - name given to a section of window or used to refer to entire window made of a number of casements. Normally, casement windows contain both opening and fixed sections.

Cavity wall - wall composed of two layers. In effect two walls separated by cavity or void. Common in construction of external walls of modern homes.

Caulk - flexible filler supplied in tube and dispensed from a sealant gun. Must be smoothed to finish before it dries. Normally acrylic or water based.

Chipboard - flooring material made of compressed wood fibres, supplied in sheets. Sheets normally joined with tongue and groove mechanism.

Concrete anchor - screw designed to fix into masonry without the need for a wall plug.

Cutting in - term used to describe painting in the corners, or at the different junctions on a wall surface, or between walls and wooden mouldings (such as architrave).

Dead lock - locking system on door which requires a key to open. Some may require a key to be put in the locked position, while others may be locked without a key but still require one for opening purposes

Door lining - wooden lining used to make up the internal part of a door frame.

Door stop - strip of wood which runs around the internal part of a door frame or lining and acts as a barrier for the door edge to close on to.

Dry lining - technique combining plasterboard and jointing compound to create wall or sealing surface ready for decoration. Jointing compound is used to cover area between sheets of plasterboard.

En-suite - term normally applied to bathroom directly adjacent to, and serving, one particular room. Usually created by building a stud partition wall in a larger room, or by converting an existing smaller room and then knocking through to the larger room.

Escutcheon - small plate used as decorative finish to a keyhole. May have a cover for insulatory/ privacy purposes.

External corner - the corners which extend out into the room.

Flush door - type of door, available in both hollow or solid forms.

Head plate - horizontal wooden stud that creates a ceiling fixing for stud wall framework.

Internal corner - the corners which point away from the centre of the room.

Jointing compound - similar to plaster or filler and used to join gaps between plasterboard when dry lining.

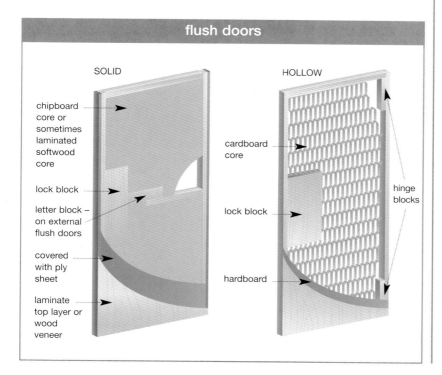

flush doors

SOLID

chipboard core or sometimes laminated softwood core

lock block

letter block – on external flush doors

covered with ply sheet

laminate top layer or wood veneer

HOLLOW

cardboard core

lock block

hardboard

hinge blocks

Jointing tape - tape used to join plasterboard sheets prior to dry lining or plastering. Self-adhesive varieties available.

Joist - length of wood used in construction of ceilings and floors.

Joist detector - sensor device used for finding the position of joists in ceilings or walls. Some may also have a different mode used to trace the position of electric cables or pipes.

Joist hanger - metal bracket used to bear the weight and position of joist ends in ceiling structure.

Junction box - box in which electrical cables are joined together.

Latch - retractable lever which allows doors to open and close into a frame

Lath - wooden laths are lengths of wood used in the make up of old walls before the invention of plasterboard. Plaster laths are small plasterboard sheets.

Leading edge - vertical edge of door or window furthest from the hinges

Lever handle - handle designed in shape of horizontal bar. Pushed down to operate latch in door

Lever latch - latch mechanism of door operated by lever handle

Lintel - support inserted above windows, doors or openings in walls.

Light - another word for casement when referring to a window section. Normally used to describe small parts of a window, either fixed or opening, e.g. 'the small light in a casement window' would be referring to a small opening section. Term also used in conjunction with windows containing lead i.e. lead light windows.

Locking lever latch - latch mechanism with separate locking system built into overall latch casing.

Mdf - or medium density fibreboard. Wooden based building board made from compressed wooden fibres.

Mitre - angled joint, which normally involves two lengths joining at a right angle so that each piece needs to be cut at a 45 degree angle.

Moulding - length of plaster or wood used as a detail to create a decorative finish on both wall and door surfaces.

Needle - length of wood inserted through hole in loadbearing wall in order to support weight of wall before the lintel is positioned. Needle is held in place by steel props at either end.

Nogging - small length of wood used in ceiling, wall and floor structure to strengthen joist framework

Open plan - home design where rooms are spacious, or where smaller rooms have been knocked into one large one.

Party wall - shared wall dividing two properties.

Plasterboard - plaster layer compressed and enclosed, or sandwiched between, thick paper, and manufactured in sheets to be used as standard building board for plaster surfaces or dry lining.

Plasticiser - a mortar additive which makes mortar more easy to use and work with.

Ply - thin veneers of wood bonded together to create building board. The grain of alternate layers or veneers tend to run at right angles to one another.

Polishing - technique of finishing a plastered surface with a plastering trowel or float.

Pva - short for polyvinyl acetate, an all purpose adhesive used to bind and/or stabilise surfaces. Used in concentrated and dilute forms.

Proprietary - referring to a material, tool, or technique which relates specifically to one manufacturer or group of manufacturers.

needles and lintels

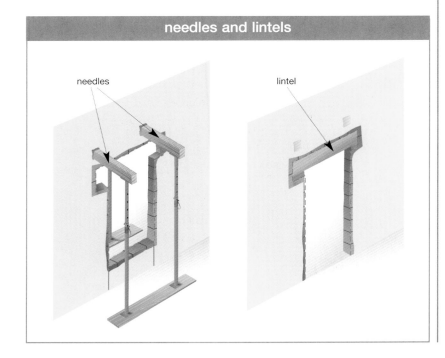

needles

lintel

Pvc - short for polyvinyl chloride, this is a general term normally used in conjunction with window make-up. However, modern pvc windows are more accurately referred to as upvc, with the 'u' standing for unplasticised. This more modern material does not de-nature in a way that some pvc windows have demonstrated.

Render - mortar based coat used internally as undercoat for plaster on solid block walls. Externally it may be used to form the finished surface, left untreated or painted as required.

RSJ - or rolled steel joists, are in essence heavy duty lintels used mainly when a loadbearing wall is removed and two rooms are converted into one.

Sash - type of window or one section of a sash window.

Scrim - traditional type of jointing tape used to cover joints between plasterboard sheets.

Sealant - any tubed silicone or mastic used for sealing joints, such as those between walls and window frames.

Skew - nailing or screwing at an angle through wood or masonry in order to provide a fixing.

Skim - applying top coat of plaster to wall surface.

Skirting board – decorative wooden moulding applied at base of wall.

Sole plate - wooden stud creating base or floor fixing for partition wall.

Solvent based - or oil based. Term used when referring to the make up of paint or glaze.

Spindle - metal bar, normally square in section, which extends from one side of the door to another through the latch casing, with each end inserted into door handles. Thus essential part of mechanism which transfers handle movement to operating the latch, so opening and closing the door.

Split level - where a room has a step in either floor or ceiling levels.

Strike plate - metal plate situated on door lining which accommodates the latch, and lock if appropriate, when the door is in a closed position.

Stud - wooden uprights used in the construction of a stud wall.

Stud wall - wall consisting of wooden studs and covered in plasterboard. Used as partition wall in houses. Finished with plaster or dry lined.

Subsidence - foundation problems in a house which cause serious cracks and movement in its structure.

Wall tie - joins internal and external layer of a cavity wall together.

Weatherboard - length of wooden moulding fixed at base of external doors to divert water away from the base of the door.

pvc and sash windows

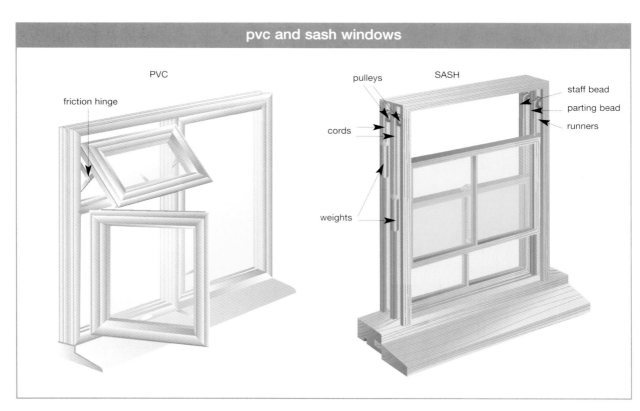

PVC

friction hinge

SASH

pulleys

staff bead

parting bead

runners

cords

weights

index

useful contacts

suppliers

A & H Brass
Tel. 020 74021854
(window and door furniture)

Area South Planning
Maltravers House
Petter's Way
Yeovil BA20 1AS
Tel. 01935 462760

B&Q DIY Supercentres
Tel. 0845 3002902

Dulux Decorator Centres
Tel. 0161 9683000

Focus Do It All
Tel. 0800 436436

Great Mills
Tel. 01761 416034

Hewden Plant Hire
Tel. 0161 8488621

Homebase Ltd
Tel. 020 87847200

Lafarge Plasterboard Ltd
Marsh Lane
Easton-in-Gordano
Bristol
BS20 0NF
Tel. 01275 377773

Magnet Ltd
Tel. 0800 9171696
(windows and doors)

MGR Exports
Station Road
Bruton
Somerset
BA10 0EH
Tel. 01749 812460

New Look Windows (SW) Ltd
West Street
Somerton
Somerset
TA11 6NB
Tel. 01458 272555

The Paragon Door and Window Co.
Unit 5
Edenbridge Trading Centre
Hever Road
Edenbridge
Kent TN8 5EA
Tel. 01732 500501

Travis Perkins Trading Co. Ltd
Tel. 01604 752424
(building materials)

Screwfix Direct
Tel. 0500 414141
www.screwfix.com
(tools and fixings)

Woods Insulation Limited
Tel. 0800 9173926

associations

**National Home Improvement
Council**
Tel. 020 78288230

Brick Development Association
Tel. 01344 885651

British Cement Association
Tel. 01344 762676

The Ready Mixed Concrete Bureau
Tel. 01494 791050

**Timber Research and
Development Association**
Tel. 01494 563091

British Woodworking Federation
Tel. 020 76085050

Hire Association Europe
Tel. 0121 3777707
(equipment hire)

Builders Merchants Federation
Tel. 020 74391753
*(advice on building materials
and lists of suppliers)*

**Draught Proofing Advisory
Association Ltd**
Tel. 01428 654011

**The British Wood Preserving and
Damp Proofing Association**
Tel. 020 85192588

Master Locksmiths Association
Tel. 01327 262255

**British Security Industry
Association**
Tel. 01905 21464

Federation of Master Builders
Tel. 020 72427583

Institution of Structural Engineers
Tel. 020 72354535

Royal Institute of British Architects
Tel. 020 75805533

Electrical Contractors Association
Tel. 020 73134800

Health and Safety Executive
Tel. 0541 545500

the authors

Julian Cassell and Peter Parham have run their own building and decorating business for several years, having successfully renovated a variety of large and small scale properties around the UK. These award winning authors have written a number of books covering all aspects of DIY, and their innovative approach has made them popular television and radio guests.

acknowledgements

We would like to thank the following individuals for supplying props, advice and general help throughout the production of this book – Adrian Moore, Steve Harris, Nick Pennison, Gary Woodland, Michael and Sue Read, Mike O'Connor, Craig Rushmere, John and Margaret Dearden, and June Parham.

At Murdoch Books (UK) special thanks are due to Angela Newton, Laura Cullen, Helen Taylor, Natasha Treloar, Joanna Chisholm and Iain MacGregor for their total professionalism and unerring ability to deal with any problem we threw at them.

Once again, Tim Ridley and Katrina Moore made all the photographic sessions a pleasure to attend, and a big thank you to them for their long hours, good humour and patience shown throughout the project. Finally, many thanks to Adele Parham for feeding the troops at a moment's notice and always being on hand to counsel two manic authors.

The Publisher would like to thank the following: Magnet Ltd, Screwfix, and A&H Brass Ltd.

First published in 2001 by Murdoch Books UK

Copyright© 2001 Murdoch Books (UK) Ltd

ISBN 1 85391 864 4

A catalogue record for this book is available from the British Library.

All photography by Tim Ridley and copyright Murdoch Books (UK) Ltd except: p8 bottom right (Murdoch Books®/Meredith), p10 and p11 (Murdoch Books®/Meredith), p22 and p23 (Murdoch Books®/Meredith), p24 and p25 (Elizabeth Whiting Associates), p30 (Corbis), p31 bottom left (Corbis), p32 and p33 (Corbis), p67 main picture (Elizabeth Whiting Associates), p78 and p79 (Magnet Limited), p91 main picture (Magnet Limited), p98 and p99 (Murdoch Books®/Meredith), p100 bottom left (Murdoch Books®/Meredith), p100 top right (Elizabeth Whiting Associates), p101 top left (Murdoch Books®/Meredith), p101 bottom left (Elizabeth Whiting Associates), p109 main picture (Elizabeth Whiting Associates), p112 and p113 (Murdoch Books®/Meredith), p125 main picture (Elizabeth Whiting Associates), p129 main picture (Murdoch Books®/Meredith)

CEO: Robert Oerton

Publisher: Catie Ziller

Publishing Manager: Fia Fornari

Production Manager: Lucy Byrne

Group General Manager: Mark Smith

Group CEO/Publisher: Anne Wilson

Commissioning Editor: Iain MacGregor

Design Concept: Laura Cullen

Senior Designer: Helen Taylor

Project Editors: Angela Newton, Natasha Treloar, Alastair Laing

Photographer: Tim Ridley

Stylist: Caroline Davies

Illustrations: John Woodcock

Colour separation by Colourscan, Singapore

Printed in Singapore by Tien Wah Press

Murdoch Books (UK) Ltd,
Ferry House, 51–57 Lacy Road,
Putney, London, SW15 1PR
Tel: +44 (0)20 8355 1480, Fax: +44 (0)20 8355 1499
Murdoch Books (UK) Ltd is a subsidiary of
Murdoch Magazines Pty Ltd.

Murdoch Books®,
GPO Box 1203,
Sydney, NSW 1045, Australia
Tel: +61 (0)2 4352 7025, Fax: +61 (0)2 4352 7026
Murdoch Books® is a trademark of
Murdoch Magazines Pty Ltd.